Praise for *Seven Practices of a Mindful Leader*

"As the former head cook of a world-renowned Zen center and cofounder of a mindfulness program at Google, Marc Lesser offers the perfect recipe for genuine conscious leadership. With his humility, vast experience, and engaging, accessible style, Marc skillfully shows how to apply the key ingredients of mindfulness to the workplace to bring out the best in others while creating an environment that both fulfills and nourishes success. A significant contribution. Enjoy the feast!"

— **JAMES BARAZ**, cofounder of Spirit Rock Meditation Center and coauthor of *Awakening Joy: 10 Steps to Happiness*

"Marc Lesser's *Seven Practices of a Mindful Leader* is a wonderful explanation of mindfulness practice, covering the skills to cultivate compassion and empathy, clarity and self-awareness, and a deeper connection to one's neighbor. While it's written mainly for executive leaders, anyone wanting a mindfulness practice in their life will find this book extremely helpful."

— **SHARON SALZBERG**, author of *Lovingkindness* and *Real Happiness*

"Marc Lesser provides an essential guide for leaders seeking to close the gap between the way they are living, working, and leading and their highest aspirations for how they wish to live, work, and lead. Marc's experience as a practitioner and teacher of Zen as well as his long-standing experience working with companies such as Google, SAP, and many other influential global organizations come together in this valuable book. It provides practical ways to hone leadership skills in the midst of the ever-increasing complexity and demands that all leaders face. A must-read for leaders at every level, including those who simply wish to lead themselves to more fulfilling work and a generative life."

— **RICH FERNANDEZ**, CEO of Search Inside Yourself Leadership Institute (SIYLI)

"*Seven Practices of a Mindful Leader* is an in-depth workbook for developing a more soulful approach to mindfulness. A lifetime of experience in both business and spiritual-practice environments has afforded Marc Lesser a deft way of explaining how and why living with more heart promotes effective leadership. I predict that these seven simple practices will be used by many. Thank you, Marc!"

— **NORMAN FISCHER**, Zen priest, poet, and author of *The World Could Be Otherwise: Imagination and the Bodhisattva Path*

"By bringing his decades of Zen meditation to the challenges of the modern workplace, Marc Lesser has discovered a fresh and compassionate vision of mindful leadership. For leaders of organizations large or small, these simple seven practices offer a wise and practical approach to fostering a healthy, dignified workplace and inspiring the very best in others."

— **MICHAEL CARROLL**, author of *The Mindful Leader* and *Fearless at Work*

"Here is a rare self-help/business book that squarely faces the pain of change. Marc Lesser is an experienced guide through rough spots. The seven practices he presents are the mature fruit of his own practice and, therefore, won't fail to enrich the lives of other leaders who practice them."

— **BROTHER DAVID STEINDL-RAST**, cofounder of A Network for Grateful Living

"This is a wonderful book that I highly recommend. Marc Lesser draws from his long and unique experience in both inspiring mindful leaders and showing how to bring mindfulness into organizations. I am grateful that I had the great privilege of working with Marc in training mindful leaders and mindfulness teachers, and he was a great mentor for me in starting a very successful corporate mindfulness program at SAP. Marc's deep wisdom, practical knowledge, and love for mindfulness applied in profound and yet practical ways shine through on every page of this wonderful book. His priceless knowledge is now available to everybody. This is a must-read for anyone who would like to become a better mindful leader and a more skillful teacher."

— **PETER BOSTELMANN**, director of SAP Global Mindfulness Practice

"With *Seven Practices of a Mindful Leader*, Marc Lesser has built an everyday bridge to mindfulness for all leaders who want to be more aware in their daily lives. At 1440 Multiversity, we believe mindfulness only matters when we put it to use, and these teachings show everyone seven easy steps to doing exactly that."

— **SCOTT KRIENS**, cofounder of 1440 Multiversity

"In *Seven Practices of a Mindful Leader*, Marc Lesser brings ancient Zen wisdom into the modern boardroom. The practices he introduces provide a clear pathway toward bringing more of our best human selves into our day-to-day leadership."

— **RASMUS HOUGAARD**, founder and CEO of Potential Project and author of *The Mind of the Leader*

"Nourishing reminders, Zen wisdom with heart."

— **JACK KORNFIELD**, cofounder of Spirit Rock Meditation Center

"No matter how we support life, this book will awaken us to what it means to be a wise and compassionate leader. This extraordinary book brings transparency and wisdom to our work."

— **REV. JOAN JIKO HALIFAX**, abbot of Upaya Zen Center

"*Seven Practices of a Mindful Leader* is a pitch-perfect harmony of Marc Lesser's two lifelong refrains — mindfulness practice and its utility in the world of business, practical affairs, and everyday life. Stripped of cant and mumbo jumbo, Marc's gentle explorations of 'great leadership' expand the boundaries of leadership to include the benefits of kindness and compassion to one's own life and the lives of others. There is no one — spiritual practitioner or corporate chief — who will not enjoy and benefit from this book."

— **PETER COYOTE**, author, actor, and Zen Buddhist priest

"All of us are leaders in one way or another. In this important new book, Marc Lesser applies the power of mindfulness and compassion to guiding and bringing out the best in others. Written from a profound depth of experience in both Zen monasteries and corporate boardrooms, every page sparkles with clarity, humor, and practical suggestions. A wonderful book, with a range and depth valuable for both first-time managers and top CEOs."

— **RICK HANSON, PHD**, author of *Resilient: How to Grow an Unshakable Core of Calm, Strength, and Happiness*

"We spend one-third of our lives at work, and work is the greatest source of stress in many people's lives. Over the past decade, an immense amount of research has documented the power of mindfulness practices to decrease stress and anxiety and increase one's ability to attend. Marc Lesser brings a unique combination of skills to address this situation, thanks to his training as a Zen priest, his immense experience training thousands of individuals in mindfulness, his work cofounding one of the leading programs bringing mindfulness and emotional intelligence skills to business, and his own experience as a business leader. *Seven Practices of a Mindful Leader* brings together this expertise and, I believe, will be an invaluable tool for changing the world of business by transforming its leaders."

— **JAMES R. DOTY, MD**, founder and director of the Center for Compassion and Altruism Research and Education at the Stanford University School of Medicine and author of *Into the Magic Shop: A Neurosurgeon's Quest to Discover the Mysteries of the Brain and the Secrets of the Heart*

SEVEN PRACTICES OF A MINDFUL LEADER

ALSO BY MARC LESSER

Know Yourself, Forget Yourself

Less

Z.B.A. — Zen of Business Administration

LESSONS FROM GOOGLE
AND A ZEN MONASTERY KITCHEN

SEVEN PRACTICES OF A MINDFUL LEADER

MARC LESSER

FOREWORD BY DANIEL J. SIEGEL, MD

New World Library
Novato, California

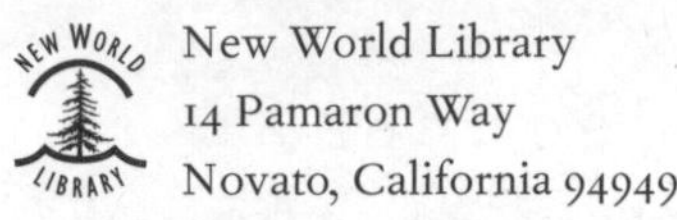
New World Library
14 Pamaron Way
Novato, California 94949

Text design by Tona Pearce Myers

Library of Congress Cataloging-in-Publication Data
Names: Lesser, Marc, date, author.
Title: Seven practices of a mindful leader : lessons from Google and a Zen monastery kitchen / by Marc Lesser, Co-founder, Search Inside Yourself Leadership Institute.
Description: Novato, California : New World Library, 2019. | Includes bibliographical references and index.
Identifiers: LCCN 2018048514 (print) | LCCN 2018050811 (ebook) | ISBN 9781608685202 (e-book) | ISBN 9781608685196 (print : alk. paper)
Subjects: LCSH: Leadership. | Mindfulness (Psychology) | Organizational behavior. | Organizational effectiveness.
Classification: LCC HD57.7 (ebook) | LCC HD57.7 .L473 2019 (print) | DDC 658.4/092--dc23
LC record available at https://lccn.loc.gov/2018048514

First printing, February 2019
ISBN 978-1-60868-519-6
Ebook ISBN 978-1-60868-520-2
Printed in Canada on 100% postconsumer-waste recycled paper

New World Library is proud to be a Gold Certified Environmentally Responsible Publisher. Publisher certification awarded by Green Press Initiative.

10 9 8 7 6 5 4 3

CONTENTS

FOREWORD

Imagine the hard-earned wisdom of a compassionate mindfulness teacher woven seamlessly with the insights of an experienced organizational leader, and you can begin to picture the illuminating tapestry of this creative and empowering book. Our inspiring guide, Marc Lesser, distills his decades of meditative practice and entrepreneurial leadership in both small and large workplace settings to provide seven powerful practices that can make our professional and even personal lives more effective and rewarding.

Lesser teaches us how loving what we do while letting go of procrastination and our attachment to unhelpful habits can free us to engage with others, our selves, and our work more productively and creatively. So much of the mind's energy is often spent avoiding discomfort — in ourselves or others — and yet learning to be compassionate and open to the inner experience at the core of who we are is the research-proven way to create healthier minds, bodies, and relationships.

"Connecting" to our own pain, the pain of others, and our

mutual interdependence are key ways in which leaders can help cultivate work environments that support optimal productivity and innovation. How? As this insightful guide beautifully reveals, being fully present in our awareness — being open to what is, as it is happening — enables us to be present in our connections with others, which helps them feel seen, safe, and secure, the basis for feeling trust. It is this sense of trust and the ensuing experience of belonging to a larger whole, to the organizational group, that a mindful leader creates, bringing out the best in coworkers in an organization, optimizing not only their productivity but also their well-being. Fortunately, these key mindful-leadership skills can be learned, and this compact book teaches exactly how to do so.

But what does being a "mindful leader" really mean? While *mindfulness* has no final and fixed definition, the term broadly means being fully present for life, opening to what is without being swept up by judgments or getting lost in efforts to cling to or avoid experiences. Being mindful entails an open awareness that creates a state of trust in which the brain's "social engagement system" is turned on and we connect with others, and even our own inner life, with more acceptance and clear thinking. A "mindful leader," then, is an individual who is able to harness these characteristics of mindful awareness in ways that inspire others to become their best selves, optimize how they solve problems, and find innovative approaches to their organization's challenges and goals. A mindful leader makes the work environment a generative social field in which compassion, connection, and creativity thrive.

The seven accessible practices in this book can teach you how to become just such a leader. This is the journey you are about to take, a journey you'll be guided on every step of the way. Enjoy!

— *Daniel J. Siegel, MD*, executive director of
Mindsight Institute and author of
Aware: The Science and Practice of Presence

INTRODUCTION

Culture eats strategy for breakfast.
— Peter Drucker

This famous quote by Peter Drucker, a world-leading business management writer, teacher, and consultant, may be one of the best-known and least-disputed aphorisms of business. It captures the truth that company culture is ultimately more important than business strategy for achieving success, and the wisdom of this statement has only become more relevant in today's tumultuous business environment.

What makes up company culture? People. Human beings working together to solve problems. I sometimes call this the "dirty little secret" of the business world, one that's easy to lose sight of in the midst of the daily pressures, anxieties, and busyness that so frequently overwhelm us. Business is people working together, and business success depends on how well we interact, collaborate, communicate, and care for one another. That's the essence of what Drucker means.

I think we recognize this, and further, I think this is what we search for, both in the workplace and in general in our lives. We want to create and be part of a supportive, positive culture — a culture of real trust and care, of transparency and integrity, of accountability and achieving results. This type of culture helps us as individuals and collectively to act with clarity, to not hold back, to show up as fully and completely as possible in all our relationships, to flourish and grow, to better serve others, and to reach our goals.

Achieving this isn't easy. Being human isn't easy. Working with others can be immensely challenging. Some difficulty always arises, whether that's painful emotions, stress and uncertainty, budgets and deadlines, interpersonal conflicts, political and marketplace strife, or the unexpected obstacles that appear whenever we pursue meaningful work.

So what do we do? How do we create and sustain what everyone says we need?

In this book, I explore these questions, and I hope to guide and inspire you using the seven practices of mindful leadership that I teach to executives, entrepreneurs, engineers, doctors, teachers, and everyday people around the world. In recent years, mindfulness and mindful leadership have exploded in popularity, but interest in mindfulness does not necessarily translate into becoming a mindful leader. Understanding mindfulness can be challenging; even more difficult is embodying and regularly practicing it in everyday life. In addition, what mindfulness means and how it's practiced can sometimes get watered down in the context of work, when it isn't dismissed altogether. Of course, ancient contemplative practices weren't developed in order to improve business. They are meant to shift our consciousness and way of being in the world. Yet these practices are essential to mindful leadership and to creating the type of supportive organizational culture that allows businesses and people to thrive.

My experience is somewhat unconventional. For most of my adult life, I've had one foot in the contemplative world and one foot in the business world, and my approach to mindful leadership has been shaped by both: from my experience as a longtime Zen practitioner and meditation teacher and as a leader, trainer, and consultant helping businesses cultivate mindful leadership and workplace well-being. Most recently I helped create the Search Inside Yourself mindfulness-based emotional intelligence program inside of Google, and I co-founded and led the Search Inside Yourself Leadership Institute, which has become one of the world's most prominent leadership training companies.

This book's seven practices were developed within the Search Inside Yourself program. One thing this experience has taught me is that people are drawn to mindfulness practice in the business world for the same reasons people practice mindfulness and meditation within any contemplative tradition — to transform their lives; to become more aware, focused, and flexible; and to shift from a narrow, egocentric, fear-based way of being to becoming more open, curious, connected, and able to help others. People seek these capacities to help them in every context and relationship, at work and outside of work.

However, the seed for these practices and for my approach to mindful leadership was sown long before, during the ten years I lived, worked, and practiced at the San Francisco Zen Center. These included two years at the City Center in San Francisco, three years at Green Gulch Farm, and five years at Tassajara, the first Zen monastery in the Western world, which is located in the Los Padres wilderness in Central California.

At Tassajara, and in the Zen tradition, work is viewed as a vital part of integrating meditation practice with daily life; work is a place of service and a container for continual learning. My first summer at Tassajara, I was the kitchen's dishwasher, and in following years I joined the kitchen crew, becoming the bread baker and the assistant to the head cook. Then, when I was twenty-eight years old, I found myself as the head cook in the Zen monastery's kitchen — aspiring to practice and embody mindfulness and mindful leadership as I supervised up to fifteen people in the daily preparation of meals for the center's seventy residential students and the seventy to eighty overnight guests.

Every day during the summer guest season, our task was to make three simple vegetarian meals for the students and three gourmet-quality vegetarian meals for the guests. Standards and expectations were, and remain, high. Tassajara has a more than fifty-year tradition and reputation for serving delicious, wholesome, and creative food, and it was the foundation from which Greens Restaurant of San Francisco originated, which is still regarded as one of the world's finest vegetarian restaurants.

Nevertheless, though I was responsible for overseeing a restaurant-quality kitchen and feeding all the students and guests, my primary responsibility was to support a culture of mindfulness practice. My main job was to support a culture in which everyone in the kitchen worked with a sense of urgency, focus, generosity, confidence, and composure. In other words, as the head cook, I had twin goals: to create a radically supportive, loving, and productive work environment and to provide great meals (on time). Neither goal could be sacrificed for the other.

In fact, in a Zen monastery, the kitchen is a central hub of mindfulness practice, and it sits in close proximity to the other central hub, the meditation hall. The kitchen and the meditation hall are considered profoundly interconnected places, places of embracing effort and effortlessness, self and selflessness; places that build community; places for expressing and celebrating care, sustenance, and spirit. The kitchen is a place of work and a place of working together — so that everyone is fully supporting and supported by everyone else — and it is also a place to bring the spirit, awareness, and approach of meditation into the world of activity.

As head cook, I found that most of the time what appeared to be two activities felt like one activity — while being present, aware, and caring for people, we made food and ran the kitchen. Other times, the goals of mindfulness and the need to get things done felt competing, as if we couldn't achieve both and had to prioritize one over the other. All restaurant kitchens, even Zen kitchens, are fast-moving, dynamic, and stressful environments. They involve lots of prep work with detailed and often complex processes, teams working together in close quarters, shifting priorities, and tight, interconnected, sometimes unreasonable deadlines. Particular to Tassajara's kitchen is that the staff are all Zen students and not professional cooks or kitchen workers. The location is remote — during my time as head cook, if we ran out of anything, whether that was not having enough eggs or any other key ingredient, the nearest store was more than two hours away. So we had to adapt and improvise. In addition, the kitchen had no electricity. Everything was prepared by hand.

I look back and wonder how we were so successful. I remember one summer afternoon I sat at a table with a group of guests I had not met as we ate lunch in the guest dining room. A woman across from me introduced herself as a graduate business school professor, and her first question was, "Who is the brains behind this operation?" She had never been to Tassajara before, and she was impressed by the quality of the food, the quality of the service, and her overall experience. In many ways, to visitors, Tassajara looks much like a well-run business conference center. I responded that the brains behind this business was that the people working here didn't view it as a business. Tassajara is a place of practice, of service, of cultivating mindfulness — which means letting go of wanting things to be different than they are and bringing awareness to one's full, moment-to-moment experience.

Today, I regard the Tassajara kitchen as a model for what mindful work and mindful leadership mean in any context, of how we can experience great joy and great love right in the midst of pressure, exhaustion, and overwhelm. The monastery's foundation and integration of mindfulness practice provided an essential context and container for everything we did in the kitchen. There was something almost magical about the level of care, learning, and playfulness, not to mention the joy and satisfaction of providing sustenance for the people we served.

It is possible for mindfulness practice, work, and leadership to be contextualized as one activity, right in the midst of many activities. This requires self-awareness, awareness of others, awareness of time, and awareness of the quality of one's efforts. Mindful work and mindful leadership both require and cultivate the essential skills we need to thrive, and this dynamic is the guiding principle of this book. In it, I have distilled what I have learned across the breadth of my experience into seven core practices that I hope will help you merge mindfulness and leadership in your everyday work life. In addition, I know that the benefits of meditation and mindfulness support our entire well-being, far beyond the needs of the workplace. They help us thrive in any endeavor.

BIG MIND AND SMALL MIND

The idea of mindful leadership is not exactly new. In an essay entitled "Instructions to the Head Cook," Dogen, the founder of Zen in Japan during the thirteenth century, advised that the head cook embrace three core practices or "three minds" while leading the kitchen. These are Joyful Mind (the mind that accepts and appreciates everything), Grandmother Mind (the mind of unconditional love), and Wise Mind (the mind that can embrace the reality of change and be radically inclusive).

Mindfulness practice itself originated within rich spiritual traditions that have developed and transformed over thousands of years. Historically, people tend to be drawn to mindfulness practice during times of rapid change, which are accompanied by high levels of stress, volatility, and uncertainty; times much like those we live in right now. In addition, over the centuries, mindfulness has been adapted and integrated to meet the most vibrant and pressing needs of society — not only influencing spiritual traditions but seeping into many facets of daily life and culture, including the arts, food, education, work, and beyond.

While it's true that increasing self-awareness is a key aspect of mindfulness practice, the intent is more than awareness of one's individual self. The intention is to cultivate a wider and more inclusive perspective, aspiring to loosen concern about oneself and to expand our narrow personal experience, so we adopt a more universal and less dualistic awareness. This is referred to in Zen as a shift from Small Mind to Big Mind.

Much of what we experience on a moment-to-moment basis is the world of Small Mind — of the personal self, of I, me, and mine. In fact, science now has a name for Small Mind — it's called the default mode network. This is the part of the brain that is often worrying about the future or ruminating about the past, rather than being relaxed and alert to this moment, to seeing with greater clarity. From a psychological perspective, this is a lot like ego. Mindfulness practice includes learning from and appreciating Small Mind while cultivating Big Mind — the more open, curious, and accepting perspective or way of being. You might say that mindful leadership is about applying the experience of Big Mind, which is cultivated through meditation (but can be accessed anytime), to the concerns of Small Mind, or the pressures and joys of daily life and of working with others to accomplish time-sensitive goals.

After my year as head cook, I was asked to be director of Tassajara, and this further deepened and broadened my experience in mindful leadership. Tassajara, in addition to being a Zen monastery, has many of the challenges common to a small business. For one thing, Tassajara's revenue provides crucial financial support for the San Francisco Zen Center. It is also, during the summer months, a retreat center — with workshops and overnight guests.

Then, after a year as Tassajara's director, I decided to leave the monastery to earn a master's degree at New York University's Graduate Business School. I was eager (as well as terrified) to enter the business world and test what I was learning about integrating mindfulness, work, and leadership. By then, I felt I'd identified several noticeable benefits to this approach, which are as follows:

- Mindful leadership cultivates a richness of experience; ordinary, everyday work can feel heightened, meaningful, and at times extraordinary.
- It removes gaps between mindfulness practice, work practice, taking care of people, and achieving results.
- It considers learning from stress, challenges, difficulties, and problems to be an integral part of the process of growth and not something to be avoided.
- It helps us recognize and work with contradictions and competing priorities to cultivate flexibility and understanding.
- It helps us experience timelessness, effortlessness, and joy even in the midst of hard work and exceptional effort.
- It can be applied to any activity to cultivate both confidence and humility.
- It embraces individuality and unity — everyone has a particular role and yet all make one team, supported by and supporting one another, practicing together.
- It considers true success twofold — in the character and compassion of the people and in the quality and results of the work.

I've since found these benefits of mindfulness practice and mindful leadership to be enduring and universal; they are accessible and available in any situation and to anyone. You don't need to spend time in a Zen monastery. You don't need a business degree. All you need is to apply the approach of mindful leadership to whatever situation, challenge, organization, role, or work environment you are in.

Mindfulness is a way of being and of seeing that shifts our perspective. It is pragmatic — endlessly so, in my experience — since it helps us solve everyday problems in effective and efficient ways. It also develops our way of being, adding depth and richness to the experience of life itself. With mindfulness, every task is approached with both humility and confidence, with hope and with letting go of hope. Ultimately, mindfulness is mysterious, plunging into questions of consciousness, birth, death, and impermanence — while providing us with direct experience that, when we let go of our fears and habits, what arises is composure, a deep sense of love, and a profound sense of meaning and connectedness to life.

PAIN AND POSSIBILITY: THE EMPOWERMENT OF MINDFULNESS

Ever since graduating from New York University, I have been part of both worlds, the contemplative world and the business world — though, of course, now I consider these one world. A few years after graduating, I founded a publishing company, Brush Dance, which became a leader in creating and distributing environmentally friendly, inspirational greeting cards and calendars. (We were one of the first companies in the world to make products from recycled paper.) I ran Brush Dance for fifteen years, and then I founded ZBA Associates, a consulting company that trains leaders and employees in using mindfulness and emotional intelligence. One of my consulting clients was Google, which eventually led to my involvement in developing the Search Inside Yourself program.

I feel fortunate that my work focuses on helping individuals, teams, and companies become more conscious and aware, as well as helping them cultivate productivity, leadership, and well-being in their work. I've been doing this in one form or another for much of my life. Nevertheless, while mindfulness as a workplace skill has become more accepted, I'm still often asked: *Why do executives and companies work with you? What motivates them to explore mindfulness?*

I usually answer this question with two words: pain and possibility. It can be painful to step outside of our role and to be more in touch with our vulnerability, with the tenderness of our heart. Additionally, we usually sense when our values, aspirations, and work are not in alignment or when we are not living up to our full potential. For example, it hurts to become aware that we avoid conflict and difficulty, or we overreact in challenging situations, and thus tend to undermine our effectiveness and influence. On the other hand, we also recognize that we are capable of acting in better, more effective, and skillful ways. We see possibility and are inspired to realize that potential.

Simply recognizing a gap between how you are living, working, and leading and how you aspire to live, work, and lead can be profound and transformative. Equally inspiring is acting to narrow these gaps in effective, practical ways. Mindfulness helps us in both efforts. It helps us identify and bridge these gaps. In fact, I think just naming these gaps can be a great gift, to feel both pain and possibility: the pain of some portions of your life right now, and the possibility for greater awareness, satisfaction, ease, effectiveness, and connection. To me, recognizing, engaging with, and learning from pain and possibility, seeing the gaps that exist, is both a core mindfulness practice and an essential leadership practice. In my trainings and workshops, this is a framework I use for understanding and practicing mindful leadership, and it is a primary approach of this book.

That said, becoming aware or more conscious of the pains and possibilities of our experience, of what is actually happening — whether that's in the world of work, community, family, relationships, or spirituality — is inconvenient and uncomfortable! It can be frightening and disruptive. This is why mindfulness, and mindful leadership, is more difficult than it may seem on the surface. Yet this is where our true power lies — our power to learn, change, and grow. This is where our ability to respond effectively, to connect deeply with others, to find solutions to problems, and to think and act creatively originates.

Signs of missed potential and opportunity are often easy to see if we dare to look. Are you avoiding facing reality or what is painful? Is your life out of alignment with your values and aspirations? Are you undermining your potential or giving away your power — that is, your ability to develop yourself, to see more clearly, and to influence others toward greater understanding, satisfaction, connection, and productivity? If so, how, or in what ways? I've posed this question — *How do you give away your power?* — to hundreds of people from many walks of life, and here are some of the answers I've received. Are any familiar to you?

- I say yes when I mean no.
- I rush from one thing to another to get to the "important" stuff and don't appreciate what I am doing in the moment.
- I overthink decisions, and then overthink my overthinking.

- I feel helpless and hopeless in light of what's happening in our world today.
- I get impatient and frustrated with myself and others over petty issues.
- I underestimate my abilities.
- I don't make clear requests or ask for help — either because I feel like I need to do everything myself or I am afraid that others won't respond to my needs.
- I avoid expressing strong emotions and often ignore my gut feelings regarding what I want or what I believe is right.
- I talk to fill space, fearing an uncomfortable silence.
- I check email, social media, or find other distractions when I feel the least bit sad or anxious.
- I am critical of myself for making mistakes or for making decisions that don't turn out well.
- I don't consistently take care of myself — I don't get enough exercise, enough sleep, or enough healthy food.
- I avoid having deep conversations or discussing topics that make me feel vulnerable.
- I compare myself to others when it comes to appearance, money, and status.
- I sometimes feel like a failure, stuck in the gap between where I am now in my work and life and what I know in my heart is possible.

These are difficult, challenging problems for anyone, yet we sometimes feel them most acutely when we are in positions of leadership, when others depend on us and have high expectations of us. These statements often represent entrenched underlying patterns and habits. There are no quick fixes to resolve or transform them. However, just the act of naming how you give away your power can be very empowering! This is the power of awareness, the power of mindfulness practice.

MINDFUL LEADERSHIP BENEFITS THE "FULL CATASTROPHE"

In this book, I primarily address business and work life, but the truth is, the seven practices of mindful leadership can benefit all aspects of our lives. Of course, we are each of us in charge of our own lives. But more to the point, gaps we identify at work, whatever our job, often relate to gaps we experience at home, in relationships, as parents, and so on. Gaps of pain and possibility exist in every realm, and sometimes, when we recognize a gap in one area, it can open up a flood of recognition that goes far beyond our original focus.

I often begin mindfulness trainings by pairing up participants and having them address two questions: What do you love about your work, and what are your biggest challenges? Afterward, I ask the group what they discussed, and at a recent training, a woman in her midforties stood up and said, "I just changed jobs, and my commute each way is now more than an hour. I feel tremendous pressure at work to perform at a high level and to learn new skills. I work with teams globally and am constantly challenged by working in multiple time zones and an array of cultural differences. I'm expected to respond to emails and texts, regardless of what time it is. I have two young children who recently started school and need a good deal of attention, and I have a husband who also recently changed jobs."

Because of her vulnerability, the clarity with which she spoke, and the familiarity of the challenges she faced, this woman had everyone's attention. We could all feel and relate to her pain. And yet here she was, taking two days out of her already overscheduled life to explore mindfulness, emotional intelligence, and leadership. Clearly, she came to this training because she sensed the possibility that she was capable of working and living differently, and everyone else there did, too.

This woman was exploring mindful leadership in part because of her work and the almost exploding demands she was experiencing as a manager. But she clearly wanted to integrate mindfulness in all areas of her life. Her description reminded me of the book about mindfulness by Jon Kabat-Zinn, *Full Catastrophe Living*. The phrase comes from the novel *Zorba the Greek*. At one point, a young man asks Zorba if he is married, and he replies, "Yes, I'm married. I have a wife, children, house, everything; the full catastrophe."

In our own ways, each of us has our own "full catastrophe." Our work and life situations are much more complex than even Zorba could have imagined. That said, while we at times can feel stuck in our own personal "catastrophes," we are often attached to them as well. I believe that the woman who spoke at the training wasn't looking to change any part of her life. She didn't want to let go of any of the activities that were so challenging and stressful. Instead, she wanted tools and practices, perhaps a different approach or way of being, that would improve her daily life, so she savored more and suffered less. She wanted to meet all her challenges more skillfully, whether at work, with her children, or with her husband. She wanted to close the gaps she felt.

First, I acknowledged her challenges and her pain and thanked her for her honesty and vulnerability. I also let her know that we'd be spending two days learning and practicing strategies for meeting pain and opening to possibility — the possibility of meeting and even at times savoring the challenges, as well as the possibility for finding calm and composure right in the midst of the storm. That is the promise of mindfulness: By shifting our awareness and patterns, we can learn to experience greater acceptance and at times awe and wonder right in the midst of the chaos and challenges of our lives.

MEDITATION MEANS LIVING WITH EYES WIDE OPEN

Stare. It is the way to educate our eye and more. Stare. Pry. Eavesdrop. Listen. Die knowing something. You are not here long.

— Walker Evans

When I first read this quote by photographer Walker Evans, I realized that my entire adult life I have practiced staring through meditation. I was introduced to Zen meditation when I was twenty-two years old, when I first arrived at the San Francisco Zen Center, and the experience changed my life. Meditation has been a fundamental practice for me ever since, and it is a core practice for mindful leaders.

While Evans doesn't seem to be talking about meditation, he captures it perfectly. When meditating, we *stare, pry, eavesdrop, listen.* We become aware and pay attention, both inside and out, so that we educate ourselves and "know something" worthwhile and useful. Indeed, we often meditate to see and understand what is most important, acutely aware that we are not here long.

The premise of this book is that leadership also requires this kind of staring: engaging your full awareness; engaging body, mind, and heart; and aligning your deepest values and intentions with the deepest values and intentions of others.

Strangely enough, I've found that meditation and leadership have much in common. Both mean living with our eyes wide open. As a practice, meditation sounds deceptively simple: just stopping, sitting, bringing full awareness to body, mind, and heart; letting thoughts and emotions come and go; cultivating kindness and curiosity; touching life's pains and disappointments, its joys and possibilities; cultivating an appreciation for being alive and for all of life, along with a radical sense of belonging and connection. Another way to describe meditation is the practice of being your true, authentic you by letting go of your ideas and identification with self.

Meditation helps us live with an appreciation of the power and preciousness of our human life. Meditation practice and all contemplative practices can be described as cultivating depth and sacredness in our everyday lives. This is what makes it mindful: Our practice helps us see what is going on, all our gaps, all our pains and possibilities, the full catastrophe.

Through meditation, as we stare, pry, listen, we learn to recognize, not only how to get things done, but how to get the most important things done with the least amount of resistance or unnecessary effort. We recognize what we can influence and what we can't, and so act more effectively. We connect more deeply with others and become better listeners. At times, meditation means fiercely struggling for change, and at times it means practicing radical acceptance. Meditation teaches suppleness and adaptability, confidence and humility. Perhaps most important of all, meditation helps lighten our hearts, helps us let go of cynicism, and opens us to our profound lack of separation from ourselves, from other people, and all life — which are important qualities for leadership and for life.

AVOIDANCE IS NATURAL BUT SELF-DEFEATING

At times, staring and focusing can be painful, and we usually avoid what is painful; that's a natural reaction. But this avoidance can keep us from achieving what is possible, since this requires naming and transforming what is painful. Avoidance is often one of the main obstacles to mindfulness, to mindful leadership, and to creating a supportive organizational culture.

We have to choose to stare, to open our eyes and wake up. When we don't, and when avoidance becomes a habit, we stop wholeheartedly engaging with ourselves and with life. We become numb, fall asleep to what is, and stop seeing clearly. This is more than a leadership or workplace issue. It's a universal human problem, one that's almost inherent to who we are as evolved beings: We can't see everything all the time, we naturally turn away from what causes pain, and we don't like change. Avoidance can sometimes feel like self-preservation, but it's actually self-defeating. Learning to look directly at what is, as much as possible, even when we don't want to, is a powerful skill that challenges us, changes us, and transforms our lives.

For example, I think of myself as having been asleep through much of the early part of my life. I grew up in the suburbs of New Jersey and lived what I considered a fairly "normal" life. I got good grades, played sports — bowling, golf, football, and baseball. I watched many hours of television and worked during the summers, caddying on golf courses, stocking items in a lumberyard, and working in a local hospital laundry room. The food I ate was mostly packaged and canned.

This numbness, ignoring, or turning away from anything that was uncomfortable was in place as part of my birth — my mother was highly medicated as I was entering this world, so that she would experience the least amount of pain possible — and it continued at school, where we had regular nuclear bomb practice drills, duck and cover. It included my visits to the Veterans Administration Hospital, where my father received shock treatments for bipolar disorder, which I now suspect was post-traumatic stress disorder. My father fought on the front lines in France and Germany during World War II, but along with my feelings, aspirations, and doubts, this fell into the category of things no one talked about.

I didn't know it growing up, but I was between worlds: between the world of feeling separate to emerging to a world of connection; from being asleep and unaware of my own pain and the pain around me to a world of intense feelings, tears, grief, celebration, and joy. From a world of ignoring the depths of the aspirations of my heart, pretending that everything was just fine, to a world of longing, struggling, and loving. Learning to love the "full catastrophe" of this crazy mixed-up world and the struggle of attempting to make sense of it all.

A similar narrative is at play today. We are between worlds and the need for mindfulness and mindful leadership has never been greater. I imagine that this is always true, but the stakes and intensity appear particularly profound at this juncture: Climate change, nuclear weapons, inequality, and terrorism are at the top of the list. Major changes in world economies, politics, health care, and our food and water systems are collapsing and being reborn at the same time. All are being catalyzed and transformed with this same power — the power of shifting from autopilot and denial to greater attention, awareness, and wakeful consciousness; the power of acknowledging our pain and the possibility of transforming this pain through staring, prying, not turning away.

We are beginning to wake up to what is and to what is possible. It's not easy. This awareness — of love, of gaps, of the poignancy of passing time, of the fact that we are not here long — can crush my heart. At the same time, the very experience of life, the pain and possibility of this human life in its totality, exhilarates me. Appreciating your life — seeing, accepting, and enjoying your life to the fullest, including all of its pains and possibilities — is what this book and the seven practices are all about.

THE SEVEN PRACTICES OF MINDFUL LEADERSHIP

In 1995, Daniel Goleman's groundbreaking book *Emotional Intelligence* was a catalyst that inspired businesses and executives to embrace the importance of emotional skills and competencies. Goleman's work sparked a revolution in interest in emotional intelligence that was quickly adopted by corporations worldwide and used in leadership trainings.

It's easy to understand why. Despite the fact that it is difficult to quantify or measure "emotional intelligence," we know it is essential and we recognize it when we see it. There are five key areas or competencies that make up emotional intelligence, and there is a great deal of agreement about (and research confirming) the benefits we get when we cultivate these areas:

- **SELF-AWARENESS**: knowing our internal states, preferences, resources, and intuitions.
- **SELF-MANAGEMENT**: turning compulsion into choice; managing our impulses, resources, and intuitions.

- **MOTIVATION**: knowing what is important to us, aligning with our values, and knowing when we are not in alignment with our values; cultivating resilience.
- **EMPATHY**: awareness of the feelings of others; cultivating connection and trust.
- **SOCIAL SKILLS**: cultivating our communication skills, especially listening, engaging skillfully with conflict, and leading with compassion.

All this sounds excellent. It paints an attractive portrait of the ideal business leader, and many predicted that emotional intelligence training would lead to a revolution in the workplace, creating just the type of positive corporate culture Peter Drucker and other experts say we need. What's interesting, however, is that despite the widespread adoption of emotional intelligence programs in the United States and globally, that revolution never came. Leadership, workplace environments, and employee well-being did not become transformed.

Ten years after publishing *Emotional Intelligence*, Goleman published a follow-up book, *Working with Emotional Intelligence*. In the chapter "The Billion-Dollar Mistake," Goleman describes what went wrong. Companies attempted to train leaders in emotional intelligence like any other subject, primarily through lectures and reading. They taught the concepts, and yet very few of these trainings ever practiced or embodied the concepts. Emotional intelligence programs explained a lot and did very little. People did not practice the core underlying competencies they needed to learn in order to actually shift emotional intelligence — such as focusing one's attention, exploring how individuals construct reality, and actively practicing selflessness and compassion. All these things are fundamental parts of mindfulness practice, but they were not included in emotional intelligence training at that time. Thus, without the component of practice, the revolution proved to be a failure.

THE POWER OF PRACTICE

I've always appreciated the corny joke about the out-of-town visitor to New York City who asks a stranger: "How do I get to Carnegie Hall?" Without hesitating, the stranger responds, "Practice, practice, practice."

When people ask me, "How can I bridge the gaps between where I am and where I want to be?" I'm always tempted to give the same answer: "Practice!" It's humorous but true.

Practice has several meanings, depending on the context. As the joke implies, you can't succeed at anything without practice, or learning the skills you need by exploring them over and over. Whether playing the piano or playing tennis, preparing for a performance or writing a report, you only improve through repetition. By doing. In this sense, practice is an intentional activity designed to increase learning, skill, and competency. In medicine or law, those who practice enough get to run their own practice, which refers to one's professional work. In this sense, your "practice" represents your business or your professional role, which can involve a lifetime of study and work to achieve.

During the years I spent living (and practicing) at the San Francisco Zen Center, the word *practice* referred to a way of life — it referred to the practice of meditation as well as to the expression of our deepest and most primary intentions. The aspiration was to integrate meditation and mindfulness practice with our relationships, work, and day-to-day activities. In this sense, our "practice" was our perspective. Our practice sought to integrate all our actions with our values and intentions.

I decided to name the seven competencies in this book "practices" for all these reasons. They are meant to be practiced in order to build skills and support integration. And they describe an approach, a way of life, and an expression of our deepest intentions. Through practice in each of these seven areas, we can transform pain into possibility.

Practices are values and intentions expressed in action. Practices are like habits, since they build a muscle memory over time. But they are more than good habits. Practices express our intention to transform our life toward our highest aspirations, for realizing our full potential and for helping others.

THE SEVEN PRACTICES: MINDFULNESS IN ACTION

Mindfulness can be (and has been) characterized in many different ways. However, for the purpose of training mindful leaders, I've distilled seven mindfulness practices:

- Love the work
- Do the work
- Don't be an expert
- Connect to your pain
- Connect to the pain of others
- Depend on others
- Keep making it simpler

These aren't your typical mindfulness instructions. To me, mindfulness is so much deeper and wider — so much more profound, messy, and mysterious — than is usually portrayed. To me, the point of mindfulness isn't to succeed at meditation, or to understand certain concepts, or to create inner peace by holding the busy world at bay. Rather, the point of mindfulness practice is to cultivate a more alive, responsive, effective, and warmhearted way of being within the world as it already exists and within the life you already live.

What makes mindfulness somewhat challenging to explain and understand is that it involves a certain amount of paradox. For instance, the renowned Zen teacher Shunryu Suzuki once said, "You are perfect just as you are, and you can use a little improvement." This is similar to the somewhat paradoxical goals of the woman I described earlier in the mindfulness training: She wanted her experience of everything to change (or improve) without changing (or letting go of) anything in her experience.

Thus, mindfulness practice sees and embraces two worlds at the same time: the universal and the relative, or Big Mind and Small Mind. On the one hand, the aim is radical acceptance of yourself and your experience. You are perfect as you are in the grand, universal scheme of things. Yet this is distinct from the relative world, and only here do you need some improvement. From the absolute perspective, you really are perfect, including your struggles, pains, desires, and aversions. Yet a core part of mindfulness practice is becoming familiar with your individual patterns and tendencies, your fears and dissatisfactions, and engaging with them to transform the everyday problems of life instead of ignoring them or pushing them away.

In this book, each of the seven practice chapters includes a variety of exercises, experiments, and activities to help you understand and realize the practices in your life. The seven practices also build upon one another, and I've grouped them into three categories, which I call "investigate, connect, and integrate." The first four practices focus primarily on the inner work of self-exploration and self-awareness. The second two practices focus primarily on relationships: your relationships with other people, with your work, and with the greater world. And the seventh practice focuses on integrating all of the practices. Ultimately, all seven practices work together to help you realize what is most important in any given moment and then make the most effective decisions. Altogether, they constitute a guide or workbook for developing yourself as a mindfulness practitioner and a mindful leader.

Here is a brief description of what the seven practices are all about.

INVESTIGATE

- **LOVE THE WORK:** Start with inspiration, with what is most essential. Acknowledge and cultivate aspiration — your deepest, most heartfelt intentions.
- **DO THE WORK:** Have a regular meditation and mindfulness practice. Learn to respond appropriately at work and in all parts of your life.
- **DON'T BE AN EXPERT:** Let go of thinking you are right. Step in to greater wonder, openness, and vulnerability.
- **CONNECT TO YOUR PAIN:** Don't avoid the pain that comes with being human. Transform pain into learning and opportunity.

CONNECT

- **CONNECT TO THE PAIN OF OTHERS:** Don't avoid the pain of others. Embody a profound connection to all humanity and life.
- **DEPEND ON OTHERS:** Let go of a false sense of

independence. Both empower others and be empowered by others to foster healthy group dynamics.

INTEGRATE

- **KEEP MAKING IT SIMPLER:** Let go of a mindset of scarcity. Cultivate awe and wonder. Integrate mindfulness practice and results.

THE ORIGIN OF THE SEVEN PRACTICES

I did not develop these seven practices on my own. They emerged out of the Search Inside Yourself (SIY) mindfulness-based leadership training program I helped develop at Google. This evolutionary process was integral to what these practices are and my approach to them, so I think it's helpful to tell that story.

In 2006, as a leadership consultant, one of my core clients was Google, where I was coaching several engineers on leadership and team building in regular sessions at their headquarters in Mountain View, California. One day I received a phone call from Chade-Meng Tan asking if we could meet. A few people at Google had referred to me as someone with "ten thousand hours of meditation practice, an MBA degree, and many years of leadership experience." Meng, as everyone calls him, was a Google engineer.

Meng is passionate about mindfulness and meditation, and he felt that the way to create a more peaceful world was to massively spread meditation. He decided to use the 20 percent of his variable work time (Google encourages employees to spend up to 20 percent of their time exploring projects outside of their core areas of responsibility) to create a mindfulness program and offer it at Google. Nothing like this existed at the time, and he invited me to be part of the team to develop the program.

At this point, he had gotten as far as settling upon the name: Search Inside Yourself, playing on the fact that Google's primary business is as a search engine. In addition, Meng had consulted with Daniel Goleman, Jon Kabat-Zinn, and others and felt that this mindfulness program should be structured around emotional intelligence and have a strong science component. Encouraging and exciting data now links meditation practice with changes in the brain and more skillful responses to stress and emotional challenges.

Meng invited Zen teacher and poet Norman Fischer along with Mirabai Bush, who was running an organization called the Center for Contemplative Mind in Society, to lead the first SIY program in 2007. I observed the way those two led the program and then provided one-on-one coaching sessions with each of the twenty-five participants. The next several iterations of SIY were co-led by Norman and me. The following year Meng and I co-led most of the trainings, along with Philippe Goldin, one of the world's leading scientists studying brain science and the effects of mindfulness.

The program was well received and became extremely popular within Google. Employees throughout the company were curious about meditation and immediately felt the impact of having a regular practice. The science of meditation was new and convincing, and we used it as a central part of the teaching of mindfulness; this was important to the open-minded but still fact-based Google engineers. The program struck a nerve, addressing the demanding, fast-paced Google culture by connecting the dots between meditation, mindfulness, emotional intelligence, science, and leadership skills. And perhaps most importantly, we were able to create an open and trusting environment that led to building a more caring, learning community. Participants were eager to have real, vulnerable conversations with one another, to share pains and challenges as well as possibilities. The program's reputation spread via word of mouth as program participants noticed they were becoming more skilled leaders and their overall well-being was noticeably improving. Several years later, pre- and post-self-report surveys confirmed these observations.

By 2009, waiting lists had grown, and as soon as a program was announced, it would fill up within minutes. In 2011, Meng and I decided it was time to offer Search Inside Yourself outside of Google, and the following year, Meng, Philippe, and I created the Search Inside Yourself Leadership Institute (SIYLI) as a 501c3 nonprofit organization. I was the CEO, Meng was board chair, and Philippe was the third board member.

By the end of 2012, the organization moved into its first offices in the Presidio in San Francisco. We had five full-time employees, were testing the program within a variety of organizations, and had just offered our first public program in downtown San Francisco. In 2013, in order to better meet the demand for mindfulness training within Google, we launched our first teacher training program for twelve Google employees.

An important aspect of teaching SIY includes teaching mindfulness and meditation. At an early meeting with these twelve teachers-in-training, we asked Norman Fischer to attend. As Meng spoke to the Google employees, I sat next to Norman, showed him the agenda, and pointed out that he was scheduled to speak next! Though he wasn't aware of it, he was supposed to give a talk on what is most important in teaching mindfulness. Norman calmly began taking notes on a blank piece of paper.

The notes were a list of what Norman believed were seven core principles for teaching mindfulness, and he proceeded to speak on them extemporaneously. As I listened, I knew these practices represented a powerful approach and path to the art of mindful leadership, well beyond the training of new mindfulness teachers. Afterward, I posted these practices on everyone's desk at SIYLI. I adopted them as guiding principles for establishing the type of work culture I wanted to create within the organization, for how I wanted to teach leadership, for how I wanted to show up as a leader, and for how I wanted to live my life.

I began to include these seven practices in talks I gave at Google and at mindfulness and leadership conferences around the world. In one of my early morning meditations, I envisioned these seven practices as a *manual* of mindful leadership, as something like what this book has become. As this image took shape in my mind, I phoned my friend Norman and asked for permission to use his teachings as the core of my next book.

Norman responded, "What teachings? I don't remember what they are." I read Norman the list of seven practices, and he said, "Oh, those are really good! I look forward to reading your book."

PART ONE

INVESTIGATE

PRACTICE 1

LOVE THE WORK

Love is the quality of attention we pay to things.

— J. D. McClatchy

One of the first times that I co-led a Search Inside Yourself training at Google headquarters in Mountain View, we had participants practice what we call "mindful listening" — where one person speaks and the other person just listens, without asking questions or interrupting. This is a way of taking the awareness involved in meditation practice into engaging with another person. Just listening, with your full attention, can be a great gift and an important skill in cultivating healthy communication. Whenever I instruct participants, I suggest that the person speaking experiment by being willing to risk not knowing what you will say; perhaps even surprise yourself by what you say. Taking turns, each speaker is to address or answer two questions: What brings you here today? And what really brings you here today? Each person gets a few minutes to speak, and then as a group we take several minutes to debrief the exercise, to discuss how it feels to just listen and to speak without interruption.

At that early training, I could not help but notice a young woman in the back of the room wiping away tears as she spoke to her partner. As each minute passed, her sobs became more pronounced. When everyone finished, I asked the group how they felt. What was their experience of bringing meditation into speaking and listening? The young woman who had been crying was the first person to raise her hand. She offered to the group that she was an engineer and was surprised at the depth and intensity of her feelings, which arose as she expressed why she was here at this training, and then why she was really here. The questions helped her remember what first attracted her to meditation and mindfulness practice as well as the loss and sadness she felt by how busy and distracted her life had become. During the mindful listening exercise, as she was speaking, she touched something deeply inside herself, and she felt cared about. She felt seen as a person and not just for her role. This feeling, of being seen and valued, was something she yearned for, as was proactively cultivating more connection and appreciation in her work and relationships.

INSPIRE, ASPIRE, AND CONSPIRE: BREATHING TOGETHER

It is no accident that "love the work" is the first practice of a mindful leader. The work of mindfulness practice begins with love, with deep caring. Love is where body, mind, and heart come together. Love is more than an idea and more than a feeling.

"Love the work" is an instruction that is surprisingly practical; it can help us to overcome obstacles in many situations. What we love we pay attention to in ways that are palpably unique. Our task, our "work" in any given moment, may seem difficult or boring. It may involve many contradictions, hindrances, and setbacks. When we approach it with love, we see what's important and embrace difficulties as part of the process, as necessities to be overcome. Love is the ultimate, most powerful motivator when taking action or relating to others, but it is a particularly powerful force when it comes to the practice of becoming more yourself, seeing with more clarity, and not being fooled by the illusions of deficiency or separateness.

There are many types of love. The kind I'm referring to here is much like the first step of the hero's journey as described by Joseph Campbell, which he names "the calling." The calling represents a profound shift of attention, a shift in one's way of being in the world; the calling asks us to leave the ordinary and pursue the extraordinary. In Campbell's words:

> The call of adventure is to a forest, a kingdom underground, beneath the waves, or above the sky, a secret island, lofty mountaintop, or profound dream state; but it is always a place of strangely fluid and polymorphous beings, unimaginable torments, super human deeds, and impossible delight.

Answering the call leads to a heightened state of awareness and of purpose. The hero seeks something of ultimate importance, which means achieving "super human deeds" in the face of real danger (those polymorphous beings and unimaginable torments). In stories, the hero usually travels to a magical, dreamlike realm, but the calling really represents a transformation in the way you see your role, your purpose, your situation, and the stakes.

Loving the work is this kind of calling. It asks us to approach leadership, our work, relationships, and all parts of our lives with the transformative motivation of love. This kind of love emerges from a deep place within and inspires us to risk and reach for what's most important.

The word *inspire* comes from the Latin *inspirare*, which means to breathe into. Love is something that is breathed into us and something that we bring our breath to. From inspiration comes aspiration, which also comes from the word *breathe*. Loving the work is aspirational — our aspirations, the things we yearn for and long for, are our ultimate goals, the aims of a lifetime. They form a deep intention, an enduring promise or vow, that continues to motivate us even when we complete certain tasks or fail at others. In Buddhist practice, there are two primary vows that express "the call," or this type of inspiration and aspiration:

> Beings are numberless. I vow to save them.
> Delusions are inexhaustible. I vow to end them.

These two statements, these vows, are inherently contradictory and impossible. The calling of love doesn't care. In fact, love is drawn to work that is difficult, even seemingly impossible. Love welcomes a challenging path, a path that seems impossible. After all, in many ways, we are impossible beings.

I often describe the work of meditation and mindfulness as a conspiracy, a word that literally means "breathing together." Meditation might sound like a solitary activity, but it is not, just like answering the call of mindful leadership isn't a solitary pursuit. That is, our aspirations and inspirations rely heavily on conspiring — so that we are all breathing together. So that we all conspire to support one another to become more ourselves and to help heal one another and the world. To me, this type of conspiracy embodies the culture that Peter Drucker suggests is all-important.

EXPLORING VALUES: WHAT DO YOU LOVE?

Ask yourself:

What inspires you?
What really brings you alive?
What do you aspire to?
What is most important to you?
What do you most love?

In *The Leadership Challenge*, a classic, bestselling leadership manual first published in 1987, authors James Kouzes and Barry Posner interviewed US Army Major General John H. Stanford, a highly decorated military leader who became the superintendent of the Seattle public school system. The authors asked Stanford for his advice about developing leaders, whether in the world of business, nonprofits, government, or academics. Stanford responded:

> The secret to success is to stay in love. Staying in love gives you the fire to ignite other people, to see inside other people, to have a greater desire to get things done.... I don't know any other fire, any other thing in life that is more exhilarating and is more positive than love is.

Then, to emphasize their point, Kouzes and Posner end their book by stating: "Leadership is not an affair of the head. Leadership is an affair of the heart."

I could not agree more, which is why "love the work" is the first practice of mindful leadership.

TRY THIS: I helped develop this exercise within the Search Inside Yourself training as a way to help participants explore their values, what matters to them most, and what they love the most.

In a journal or on a sheet of paper, write down the names of three people whom you most admire. They can be alive or no longer living, from your personal connections or from history. They can be fictional movie characters or even cartoon heroes. Who comes to mind? Let yourself be surprised.

Then write a sentence or two as to why you chose these three people. What have they done and what do they represent to you? Think of situations that exemplify what led you to choose them. (I suggest doing this first before reading further.)

Usually the people we choose, those we most admire, represent what is most important to us. Does that fit for you? From your descriptions of these three people, write down what you consider your top three to five values. As you reflect on what you value, other ideas may arise that aren't captured by the people you chose. You can add those as well.

Once you have your list of values, experiment with writing whatever comes to mind based on one or more of these prompts:

- What is most important to me is…
- My values are…
- The ways my values show up in my work and life right now are…
- The ways my work and life and values are not in alignment are…
- Actions I might take to narrow the gap between my values and activities include…

WHAT IS LOVE?

Love is certainly a "calling" of leadership, but it's also helpful to define love as a way to reflect on what this practice is really asking us to do.

While there are many kinds and definitions of love, I'd like to focus on four qualities or practices that make up love. In Buddhism, these teachings are known as the four immeasurables, since it is said that, as you practice them, each of these elements and the four together will continue to grow beyond what can be measured. These four qualities are:

- loving kindness,
- compassion,
- joy, and
- equanimity.

LOVING KINDNESS: This is the practice of caring about others. I remember many years ago when I was CEO of Brush Dance, I was interviewed for a magazine article on the topic of integrating business and Zen. The reporter asked me, "What does it look like to practice Zen in the workplace?" My response was that the core practice is kindness — to care about and be kind to the people I work with, to our customers, to vendors, and even to be kind to myself. The reporter was clearly not satisfied, and he said, "No, really, what does it mean to practice Zen in the workplace?" I repeated my answer, saying that kindness is more difficult than it seems, especially when things go wrong, when there are conflicts, when cash flow is challenging. Kindness goes a long way at work.

COMPASSION: Compassion has three parts: feeling another's pain, understanding others, and desiring to help others. Compassion, and leading with compassion, is a core part of mindful leadership. Compassion is a core thread that runs throughout these seven mindfulness practices.

JOY: This refers to a deep sense of happiness that is not dependent on conditions. It is the joy of appreciating being alive. This isn't the Small Mind joy of doing well at work and getting a bonus; this is the Big Mind joy that appreciates and celebrates everything, good and bad. This particular practice of joy is also sometimes translated as sympathetic joy, or the practice of feeling joy by acknowledging, feeling, and celebrating the happiness of others.

EQUANIMITY: This is the practice of letting go of self-concern, of cultivating acceptance and composure. Equanimity doesn't mean suppressing or tamping down feelings. It is the practice of finding composure right in the midst of stress, confusion, change, challenges, and urgency.

In one of the early teachings of the Buddha, he names a variety of benefits that come from cultivating these practices of love. These benefits include

- sleeping well,
- lightness in the heart upon waking,
- being well liked by others,
- being able to concentrate easily,
- that your face will be brighter and clearer, and
- at the time of death, the mind will be clear.

These are pretty great benefits! I would add that, if you practice "love the work" in these ways on a regular basis, you are more likely to be happier and the people around you will be happier. Your work will be more effective and more successful. And you will influence the culture around you to be more engaging, creative, and lighthearted.

WHAT IS "THE WORK"?

While "love the work" means bringing the intentions and perspective of love to everything we do, this practice also refers to a very specific kind of work: cultivating mindfulness. This means seeing with greater clarity what really is and letting go of whatever more limited worldview we have constructed. It means cultivating greater self-awareness in order to, paradoxically enough, become less self-centered. It means actively questioning what is with an open-ended curiosity.

To love the work is to open ourselves and notice, the best we can, the ways in which we create limited mindsets and narrow mental models. To use the terms raised earlier, it both embraces and transcends Small Mind, or our default mode network, by accessing the perspective of Big Mind. When we reduce or let go of self-referential fears and worries, we realize that wonder and connection are our true default modes of being. Loving the work recognizes that there are many realities, many ways of being, and that we should not be overly attached to our version of reality.

The work of mindfulness is to step outside ourselves in order to see ourselves and notice what we aren't aware of. We try to identify our unspoken fears, blind spots, biases, and assumptions. This means cutting through the places where we are caught, limited, attached, beholden to outmoded beliefs, and stuck in patterns or stories. By loving the work, we build trust in ourselves, we become more trustworthy, we cultivate inner strength, and we improve relationships and results.

This work requires courage. Not the physical courage required to save someone's life or fend off an attacker, but the courage to be real, open, and vulnerable. The courage to feel uncomfortable and exposed, like the Google engineer who wept openly and shared the pain that had brought her to the workshop. It's the courage to speak and take action in the midst of these feelings. The payoff is well worth it.

MEDITATION: LEARNING TO STARE, PRY, EAVESDROP

Meditation is a core practice for cultivating mindfulness. Meditation is designed to help us interrogate reality and to increase our comfort with change, difficulty, and the unknown. In recent years, this has been verified and quantified in scientific research. For instance, a 2011 study entitled "How Does Mindfulness Meditation Work?" by Britta Holzel, Sara Lazar, and others describes some of the concrete benefits of mindfulness meditation. The study's summary describes it like this:

> By closely observing the contents of consciousness, practitioners come to understand that these are in constant change and thus are transient. The mindful, nonjudgmental observation fosters a detachment from identification with the contents of consciousness. This process has been termed "reperceiving" or "decentering"...and has been described as the development of the "observer perspective."

Here's a closer look at what that means in more everyday language.

"CLOSELY OBSERVING THE CONTENTS OF CONSCIOUSNESS": An important aspect of mindfulness practice and of interrogating reality is observing our thoughts, feelings, and sensations — becoming more aware of our experience. Sometimes we feel things without fully realizing what has triggered those feelings. We also construct an identity, an "I" and a "me" with particular desires and aversions. Mindfulness is becoming intimate with our consciousness and noticing habits and patterns.

"UNDERSTAND CHANGE": By becoming familiar during meditation with the fleeting nature of our thoughts and emotions, and gaining more understanding of change, this aspect of mindfulness becomes a regular feature of moment-to-moment awareness.

"DETACHMENT FROM IDENTIFICATION": Mindfulness supports the ability to see our stories and narratives as reflecting our subjective, and not objective, reality. As the Google engineer stated, we are more than our roles, more than the persona we develop. Meditation helps us step back and observe our thinking and emotions as an outsider might. We increase our ability to see ourselves with more perspective.

"REPERCEIVING": This is related to detachment. The practice of noticing and becoming familiar with our thoughts, feelings, and perceptions helps us become less identified with them, so we can see them in a different light or perhaps in more useful and accurate ways.

Mindfulness Meditation Practice

Let's practice.

Begin by bringing attention to your body. Find a way to sit, whether you are in a chair or on a cushion, where you can be fully alert and fully relaxed at the same time.

To emphasize relaxation, start by softening the area around

your eyes and the muscles in your face. You can keep your eyes open, without focusing, or close your eyes if that feels more comfortable. Notice and if possible let go of any places you are holding or feeling any tension. Notice the transition from whatever you were doing to stopping, pausing, and letting go. Whatever you were engaged in, your projects, to-do lists, all your unfinished business — let it all go. It will be there later.

To emphasize being alert, sit up slightly straighter than you might normally sit, putting some attention to your spine, arching your back slightly. Choose how to place your hands and your feet. Open up your shoulders and chest, allowing breathing to be unrestricted. Often we restrict our breathing without being aware of this.

Right now, bring attention to whatever is happening with your body. Notice your feet touching the floor, your hands on your thighs or in your lap. Notice what it is like to be sitting in the chair or on the cushion. Relax the muscles in your jaw. Check in with the body.

Now bring attention to your breathing. Just be aware that breathing is happening, without you having to do anything. Notice each inhale and each exhale, and the spaces in between. Can you bring a sense of curiosity to breathing, a childlike quality of interest, as though you are noticing your breath for the first time? This time, this breath, is in fact new. It has never happened before and will never happen again. So pay attention! With curiosity, and perhaps a touch of warmheartedness toward yourself. Remember, a central aspect of mindfulness meditation, and of loving the work, is cultivating an attitude of openness and kindness toward ourselves.

What is happening with your thinking mind? Is your mind busy or calm, skeptical or open? Just notice, then gently bring your attention back, as much as you can, to your body and your breath.

What are you feeling? What is your mood? Again, just notice. Check in with your feelings. Perhaps go deeper and ask: *What is in my heart right now? What are my deepest, most basic feelings? What do I love?*

Bring to mind people that you most love; your partner, children, parents, or closest friends. Let yourself feel a sense of deep care, appreciation, and connection. Let go of the stories and dramas. Let yourself feel loved and appreciated. Now, see if you can widen your circle of care and love. Offer the thought: *May everyone, may all beings be happy, may they be free, may they be at peace.*

Then, keeping it simple, let go of these thoughts and gently bring your attention to your body or your breath.

Just notice: What is it like to be sitting here, right now? Without trying to change anything, can you let go of all ideas of right and wrong, and simply bring your attention to your experience? What is it like to be here right now? What is it like to be alive right now? Can you ask these questions with curiosity and with a sense of appreciating whatever arises?

Notice that sometimes you can focus — on your breath and body and feelings. Sometimes you can open your awareness to the sounds, the light, any sensations; opening your body and mind to whatever is there.

Sit quietly for a few more minutes, making just the right amount of effort to be aware.

Then, whenever you are ready, bring your attention back to your space and whatever is next for you. See if you can bring this sense of focus, openness, curiosity, and warmheartedness into your day and your life.

REFUSING THE CALL: THE THREE APES

I have always found it interesting and surprising that in Joseph Campbell's model of the hero's journey, the second stage after "the calling" is "refusing the call." In stories, the hero will get a clear calling but then immediately be filled with doubt, hesitation, or outright fear. I've found this to be true in my life. Moments of inspiration and aspiration are hard to sustain. We genuinely desire to "love the work" and practice mindful leadership, but love can be difficult and risky. Love means being vulnerable and open. Seeing clearly means acknowledging pain, failure, and limits.

Evolutionary biology tells us that the human species evolved over millions of years for one thing and one thing only — to survive and pass on our genes to the next generation. We evolved to feel fear, to be dissatisfied, and to need connection. These inherited, evolved characteristics can be barriers to love and internal obstacles to mindful leadership. In short, in most situations, our first instinct is self-preservation, and we tend to pull back when we feel at risk.

Mario, a Google scientist friend, is fond of saying, "We are descendants of the nervous apes!" The apes that were chill and relaxed, they didn't make it. They didn't survive. They were killed or eaten by predators. As descendants of the nervous apes, our tendency is to scan for threats, both external threats in our environment and internal threats. In the realm of survival, it's better to be wrong 99 percent of the time and right 1 percent of the time. This is essential when physical safety is all that matters. In that case, it's wise to treat any potential threat as a life-or-death situation.

Yet this mindset doesn't fit today's world and can be problematic. The world remains full of threats, but relatively few to our life. Yet our nervous system reacts in virtually the same way: Whether we're responding to an angry email or a hungry tiger, the same alarm bell (the amygdala) rings in our brains and our sympathetic nervous system kicks into action.

Internally, this process of scanning for threats laid the ground for our strong inner critic as well as our negativity bias. Research has shown that we often judge ourselves harshly and that we tend to experience negative emotions more quickly and with greater intensity than positive emotions. The nervous ape doesn't like to be vulnerable or ask difficult questions. Reality can feel threatening. Of course, we may truly believe that loving the work and seeing more clearly is the better approach — the true path to sustainable safety, satisfaction, and success — but the nervous ape needs calming and convincing to go that route.

We are also descendants of the imaginative apes. At some point, our ancestors developed consciousness, the ability to be present not only for whatever we are doing in the moment but to recall the past and imagine the future. Indeed, in our minds, we can conjure just about any scenario or reality we want! This is truly amazing. We not only take consciousness for granted, we rarely acknowledge the magic of our imaginations. Consciousness itself is truly astounding; it remains a mystery where it came from and all that it can do. And there's more. Our imaginations allow us to create an identity, a self. This self both influences and is influenced by a host of thoughts, feelings, emotions, assumptions, and beliefs — some based on actual events, and many based on imagined events — to form a "me," an "I," an individual life. Then, together with our families, friends, organizations, and culture, we create entire societies and worlds, which are really incredible stories of our collective imaginations — what we call laws, borders, marriage, institutions, money, and much more.

Oddly enough, despite this unlimited power to conjure, the imaginative ape is rarely satisfied. It seems that another aspect of human evolution and human nature is nearly always wanting more and better — more and better food, sex, money, status, whatever. The imaginative ape is often comparing, contrasting, judging, and thinking ahead, so we are almost perpetually focused, on some level, on what we lack relative to others or to what we want. Even when we get what we want, we can easily imagine the possibility of loss, which undermines our satisfaction. Of course, the ability to judge and plan for potential threats is a big positive for our survival, but not so much for seeing clearly. It's not as though once we have great sex or a tasty meal, we are then satiated and complete. No, these feelings and experiences of satisfaction wear off, and we start to search for more.

Thus, the imaginative ape also represents another potential obstacle on the path to mindful leadership. The good news is that we can train our imaginations to be more satisfied, more complete, more able to remain in the present moment, as opposed to ruminating on the past, imagining what we lack, anticipating negative futures, and assuming (often inaccurately) the thoughts and intentions of others.

Finally, we are also descendants of the empathic, social apes. We need connection, and we are hardwired to feel the feelings, pains, and joys of others, along with the many nuanced emotions in between. Though this ability has been understood experientially for a long time, it was first confirmed scientifically in a 1982 study done (ironically) with monkeys. Researchers at the University of Parma, Italy, discovered that neurons fire in the same area of the brain whether a person is performing an action, like eating, or merely observing someone else doing the same thing.

As with the other two, this trait is likely evolved; individual survival, and raising the next generation, is of course improved when individuals work together. Humans have a profoundly strong and primal need for connection to others. Our identities, our sense of meaning and purpose, the way we see ourselves, and the way we process thoughts, emotions, and actions — all are formed and intertwined within our relationships with family members, friends, coworkers, and all the people who make up the web of communities we are part of.

However, this puts a premium on choosing or aligning with others we can trust, understand, and communicate with, and often the need to feel safe and the need to feel connected can be at odds. The empathic ape wants to foster connections to a small group, family, or tribe, but it fears disconnection within this group. Conversely, it tends to treat anyone outside that family, tribe, or group identity as a threat.

Seen in a positive light, these "three apes" represent three core human needs: safety, satisfaction, and connection. They also make useful metaphors for our three primary centers: body, mind, and heart. Yet the three apes also tend to react first, or express themselves initially, in negative ways: The nervous ape easily feels fear for personal safety. The imaginative ape easily feels dissatisfied with self and others. And the empathic ape easily fears and fosters division.

In other words, the three apes represent the tremendous potential of human beings: (1) a strong sense of self-preservation that inspires courageous feats, (2) an incredibly advanced and developed imagination, and (3) a strong need for connection and the ability to communicate and understand emotions. But that potential cuts two ways. The same attributes that help us succeed when we feel the call of mindful leadership may also respond by refusing that call in the name of safety and self-protection.

We have the potential to live in a world of confusion, of misunderstanding — to create a world based primarily on fear and mistrust, to enhance and increase this fear using our imaginations, and to ignore our similarities and emphasize our differences. This path is likely to result in increased individual stress and unhappiness, greater inequality and separation, more misunderstanding and more violence. To our dismay, this often seems to be the world we have created, the one we are currently living in.

Or, as mindful leaders, we can cultivate love and understanding: We can acknowledge our vulnerability and tendencies to respond strongly to threats, and we can use our imaginations to calm, retrain, and transform our fears. We can cultivate more trust of ourselves. And we can acknowledge the reality of our interconnectedness by looking deeply at our profound similarities. We can see that we are all part of the human family, living on and sharing one planet. We can aspire to create another reality — the reality of trust and understanding, using our innate abilities for empathy and compassion. We can transform fear to hope and possibility and move toward creating a life of more meaning and satisfaction, of greater connection, health, and cooperation.

TRY THIS: As an experiment, consider the three apes inside yourself. Take a moment to greet and get to know them. For instance, the nervous ape: Take a few moments to bring attention to when you feel safe and when you are scanning for threats. Reflect on and relive as much as possible particular situations in recent days or weeks. Where in your body do you feel safe, and what is the feeling of scanning for threats or of feeling fear?

As for the imaginative ape, bring attention to your need for satisfaction, for food, for sex, or for distractions. Just notice: What are your thoughts that lead to satisfaction or to dissatisfaction? Again, reflect on how you interact with those you work with or people in your personal life.

Now, the empathic ape: What is it like to feel the emotions of others? Bring awareness to this ability. Bring attention to your need for connection. What supports your feeling of connection and what gets in the way? Be as specific, curious, and honest with yourself as possible. If you want, write about what you discover.

IDENTIFYING CREATIVE GAPS AND GROUND TRUTHS

The practice "Love the work" refers to answering the call of mindful leadership and developing a mindfulness practice in order to see more clearly. This sounds straightforward. Through mindfulness, our intention is to recognize change, recognize what is, and recognize our aspirations, but the three apes may feel threatened by some or all of this. We should expect to encounter and have to overcome some internal resistance, which is part of the process of seeing more clearly.

For instance, reality has an irritating habit of shifting and changing, totally undermining our hopes, dreams, and fantasies. When our ideas and plans collide with reality, reality generally wins, whether it's the reality of our aging bodies and minds, of our mercurial emotions, of upheaval in the business world, or of the shifting priorities and feelings of other people — family, friends, and coworkers.

When this happens, we may not want to admit that reality isn't going to meet our expectations, but we create trouble for ourselves if we do not. We need to see what is, or what the military calls "ground truth." This is what's actually happening, the reality of the battle or situation on the ground, as opposed to what intelligence reports and mission plans predicted would happen. The ground truth is what you say to yourself and closest friends about the reality of your experience, as opposed to what you want, or what you hoped or planned would happen, or how you'd like to appear to others.

For a moment, consider your "ground truth" in these areas:

- **YOUR WELL-BEING**, including sleep, exercise, diet, and your state of mind: What are you experiencing versus your aspirations?
- **YOUR WORK**: How's it going? What's the reality?
- **YOUR EXPERIENCE OF YOUR CORE RELATIONSHIPS**: Would you say you are satisfied or disappointed, and how?

In war and in life, there are always gaps between our ground truths and our visions of what we expected or wanted. Naturally, we'd like to close these gaps if we can, but first we have to see and acknowledge them. So, one important practice for loving the work is to acknowledge where you are right now, where you want to be, and the gaps between these two. Doing this requires being curious, appreciative, and warmhearted with yourself while at the same time "staring," looking directly at what is and what you want. This is an important, even paradoxical skill and practice: acknowledging the gaps between what is (the ground truth) and what you want, while at the same time appreciating what is without trying to change it.

In his groundbreaking book *The Fifth Discipline*, Peter Senge calls these gaps "creative tensions." He says that one of the most important skills of leadership is staying with these gaps instead of covering them over or finding strategies to make them go away in order to feel more comfortable.

TRY THIS: Having considered your "ground truth" in several areas, identify some of your core or most critical creative gaps. In what areas is the difference between what actually is and your vision of what you want the widest? What are some ways you might narrow or even close those gaps?

What support do you need?
What skillful conversations might be useful?
What has stopped you from closing the gaps up to now?
What might you need to accept rather than change?
What is there to learn?

A LEADER'S JOB IS MINDFULNESS

Another way to appreciate how well mindfulness and meditation practice serve leadership is to compare what leaders do with what mindfulness provides. Whenever I do this, I'm always struck by how closely and deeply meditation's benefits align with the needs of leadership.

There are many definitions of leadership, but in this context, I would say that leaders do essentially three things:

1. **THINK** — leaders use intelligence to plan, envision, problem solve, focus, and see from a multitude of perspectives.

2. **LISTEN** — they care about others and collaborate with others to execute a shared vision, which means being open, vulnerable, and curious.
3. **HOLD SPACE** — they try to be fully present, clear, emotionally open, and credible; they influence the culture by creating positive norms around storytelling, flexibility, and accountability.

These three leadership skills line up nicely with the three apes. The skill of thinking is an antidote to the emotional reactivity of the nervous ape. The skill of listening to others is an antidote to the sometimes false, self-serving narratives of the imaginative ape. And holding space is a way to foster inclusion and intimacy within a group, as well as to motivate a group to action, which can be challenging for the empathic ape.

Mindfulness practice is also keenly aimed at each of these activities — cultivating clear thinking, cultivating the ability to listen deeply (to yourself and others), and developing your presence, openheartedness, and responsiveness.

These effects are increasingly being quantified through research. Richard Davidson is one of the world's leading scientists studying meditation and its influence in cultivating a healthy mind. In *Altered Traits*, Davidson and coauthor Daniel Goleman describe four areas that meditation transforms:

- Recovering from stress, as well as reducing reactions to disturbing events.
- Increased empathy and compassion.
- The ability to focus and maintain focus and attention, as well as our ability to open awareness and to see from a variety of perspectives.
- The ability to loosen our sense of self and lessen

identification with ego, leading to an increased sense of lightness and appreciation.

In other words, leadership and mindfulness are both aimed at seeing more clearly and living more thoroughly in reality. Leaders are focused on the reality of the relative, ever-changing, everyday world: on the changing marketplace and workplace; on the reality of the skills, talents, minds, and hearts of the people within the organization and of the people the organization is trying to reach. In both mindfulness and leadership, part of seeing clearly is not avoiding difficulty, conflict, and pain, but addressing these in order to shift toward greater alignment and understanding. Leadership is about problem solving and inspiring and empowering others — all qualities that are directly supported by mindfulness practice.

Contained in the essential definition of these two words *mindfulness* and *leadership* is "seeing clearly." Mindfulness practice and leadership aim at seeing through our mistaken assumptions, biases, and conditioning that lead to unnecessary stress and fear so that we can realize the potential of who we already are.

However, seeing clearly means something else as well. Yes, it means acknowledging the realities of pain and impermanence, but seeing clearly also means seeing past our relative circumstances, or the world of everyday reality. Seeing clearly means experiencing yourself and the world from an absolute perspective, where nothing is lacking and where everything is radically interconnected. This type of seeing means experiencing Big Mind, which is a foundation of meditation and mindfulness and a way to become a more effective leader.

THE WAY-SEEKING MIND

The practice "Love the work" is more than an idea. The call to love the work may be profound or it may be much more ordinary, subtle, or surprising. Without noticing, you might experience a dropping away of what you previously believed was important and discover a new set of priorities.

Loving the work is a practice in the grandest sense, the devotion of a life's work, a way of being in the world. Just like the musician who plays music just because, whether they reach Carnegie Hall or not, loving the work is satisfying on its own merits and doesn't need reasons, benefits, or rationales.

What is it that brings you alive? What pulls you to want to be more aware, to help others, to make the world a better place? What brought you to mindfulness, to this book, to doing this work?

There is an expression from Zen practice called the way-seeking mind. This refers to the act of identifying the events, thoughts, and feelings that mark when a person embarks on a path of living with greater mindfulness and wholeheartedness — someone who, in this book's terms, practices loving the work. With a way-seeking mind, we aspire to cultivate more openness and understanding, to walk a path of widening awareness, to experience more depth and sacredness. That depth and sacredness is already there, and the path to living a more mindful life is simply our vow or determination to wake up to it. As Walker Evans said, we pledge to "stare, pry, eavesdrop, listen. Die knowing something."

I'm often asked what brought me to mindfulness practice. When did I begin to love the work? What led me to begin a mindfulness practice when I was in my early twenties? I have many responses, but perhaps the most accurate is that I don't know. How did a young man who grew up in a working-class home in a small town in central New Jersey end up moving to

California and living at the San Francisco Zen Center for ten years? I can't truly say, but I can point to several key events and pivotal moments.

One such event was reading *Toward a Psychology of Being* by Abraham Maslow. I was a freshman at Rutgers and feeling somewhat depressed — my first real romantic relationship had just ended — when reading Maslow was assigned in psychology class. Maslow's words about self-actualization touched me deeply. I couldn't help noticing my own pain — and how undeveloped and needy I felt — as well as my unrealized potential. Maslow helped me see what I was capable of, and I wondered, *Why isn't everyone doing this work?* This was one moment when I was called and began to love the work.

What are the key events or pivotal moments that have brought you to where you are now? When did you begin to love the work?

TRY THIS: In a journal, write down your "way-seeking mind" story. Describe what first drew you to want to be a leader, to be a better person, to live with more awareness, depth, and sacredness. Perhaps it was a moment of pain or an experience of inspiration. Describe what happened, how you felt, what you learned about yourself and your life, and where you see yourself heading. Explore both your pain and possibility.

LOVE THE WORK
KEY PRACTICES

- Ask yourself: What brings me alive, and what really brings me alive?

- Explore your values, or what you love, by naming the people you admire and the values they represent.
- Practice four types of love: loving kindness, compassion, joy, and equanimity.
- To cultivate mindfulness and see more clearly, practice meditation.
- Get to know the "three apes" inside yourself, which represent your fears, dissatisfactions, and need for connection.
- Acknowledge your ground truths and identify creative gaps: What are yours?
- Tell your "way-seeking mind" story (in a journal or to a friend). What brought you to love this work?

PRACTICE 2

DO THE WORK

The success of an intervention depends on the inner condition of the intervener.

— Bill O'Brien

If loving the work is like a calling, involving inspiration and aspiration, then practice 2, "Do the work," is acting from this love, putting what you love into action. If loving the work is the essential launching pad to mindful leadership, doing the work means being that mindful leader: having a regular mindfulness practice, embodying your values and aspirations, engaging skillfully with others, and living a life of cultivating awareness and helping others.

How do you become the mindful leader you envision? Like the Carnegie Hall joke: just practice.

At its simplest, that is all that "do the work" means. It's a reminder to have a regular practice and to integrate mindfulness into your everyday life — your leadership, work, family, relationships, and daily activities. As a practice, "do the work" means approaching everything you do as an opportunity to learn and grow, to see more clearly — to practice.

TWO TYPES OF PRACTICE: DEDICATED AND INTEGRATED

When it comes to doing the work, I like to distinguish two main categories of mindfulness practice: dedicated practice and integrated practice. These are somewhat artificial distinctions. From the perspective of Big Mind, everything we do is practice. However, in everyday terms, this can be a useful distinction. Both types of practice are important, and each supports the other.

To use a sports metaphor, dedicated practice is literal practice, time "dedicated" outside of the game to learn, to cultivate greater understanding and insight. If you're a baseball player, that means time in the batting cages: hitting a hundred balls, slowing down your swing, analyzing and adjusting it, experimenting with hitting different pitches, and so on. Integrated practice is the game: using your skills in the moment, during the heat of competition, when hitting the ball well matters.

Where this metaphor breaks down, for mindfulness, is that dedicated practice and integrated practice are often the same thing. The "game" is life and every moment matters. Also, we practice without any reason, for the sake of experiencing our aliveness, without trying to improve or seek specific benefits.

For example, several years ago I co-led a one-day Search Inside Yourself program for Google's doctors and health care providers. My coteacher was a Google employee whom I had trained as a Search Inside Yourself teacher. After introducing the topics of mindfulness and emotional intelligence, my coteacher described the process of meditation as bringing attention to the breath, noticing distraction, and then returning attention to the breath. Then he used the metaphor that "meditation is much like going to the gym." Each time you bring your attention back to your breath, you are improving your ability to focus, like strengthening a muscle as you repeat this process again and again.

I thanked my coteacher and said that while I agreed with this metaphor, it is also true that "meditation is nothing like going to the gym." My coteacher was a bit surprised. He smiled, looked at me, and said enthusiastically to the participants, "Well, that's why we have two teachers!" Fortunately, we had a really good, trusting relationship, as I had been mentoring him for the past year, and he was not put off by my contradiction.

I clarified that going to the gym implies that you are meditating to get a result and that you expect a step-by-step improvement. This can be useful, and encouraging, and it can also be a hindrance to the real power and benefits of meditation practice.

Another approach to meditation is to completely let go of all reasons and rationales for meditating, giving up any ideas or hopes of improving or getting anything. Instead, as you meditate, see what it is like to just be quiet, still, and alive, just appreciating your experience, seeing yourself and accepting yourself as you truly are. This is the approach of dedicated practice, in which meditation is more like a sacred ritual, an act of trust, believing in and expressing yourself outside of ego or expectations.

Here is what Dogen, founder of Zen in Japan in the thirteenth century, had to say about meditation practice:

> The sitting practice I speak of is not learning meditation. It is simply the gate of repose and bliss, the practice-realization of totally culminated enlightenment. It is the manifestation of ultimate reality. Traps and snares can never reach it. Once its heart is grasped, you are

> like a dragon gaining the water, like a tiger taking to the mountains.
>
> You should therefore cease from practice based on intellectual understanding, pursuing words and following after speech, and learn the backward step that turns your light inwardly.

I love Dogen's poetic description of meditation, and his deep sense of knowing, speaking from the depth of his own experience. He is saying that, in meditation, there is nothing to gain or achieve; just this act of stopping, breathing, and letting go of everything breaks down and transcends our ideas of what practice is and what realization or self-actualization are. In the Zen tradition, "take the backward step" refers to a deep sense of letting go and is the opposite of trying to gain something. It is a much-revered instruction for meditation practice, as is "it is simply the gate of repose and bliss." Of course, this might not be your (and it is not my) day-to-day experience of meditation. But why not? What gets in the way? Dogen's words are meant, I believe, to be aspirational and practical: They shift our assumptions regarding both meditation practice and our lives.

Dogen uses evocative metaphors that embody what mindfulness practice leads to: We become "like a dragon gaining the water, like a tiger taking to the mountains." This is how I aspire to show up as a mindful leader, to teach mindful leadership, and to live my life — completely in my element, with a sense of incredibly grounded confidence and radical belonging, able to be fully present and ready to meet whatever comes my way.

DEDICATED MINDFULNESS PRACTICE

Nevertheless, with those distinctions in mind, to cultivate mindfulness and become more mindful leaders, it is important to develop and sustain a dedicated mindfulness practice. This means practicing mindfulness daily separate from the needs, stresses, and activities of "regular" daily life.

Here are some examples of dedicated mindfulness practices:

- meditation,
- walking meditation,
- journal writing.

Meditation

In practice 1, I present a simple guided meditation (pages 43–45) that anyone can use and that you can adapt as you wish. Of course, there are many types, traditions, and ways to meditate; none are wrong. Yet particularly for people new to meditation, I suggest keeping your approach simple. Just take time regularly to stop and sit quietly each day, even if it's just for a few minutes.

When I am asked to describe what meditation is, and the different approaches that are used, I sometimes tell the three bricklayers story. In this tale, three bricklayers are working together, and all three appear to be doing the same activity, laying bricks. When the first bricklayer is asked what he is doing, he says exactly that: He is laying bricks. When the second is asked, he says he is supporting his family. And the third says he is communicating with God, since these bricks are part of a church they are building.

Meditation can be described like this. It looks like one activity, but it can actually be several activities. It can be just sitting and noticing body, breath, thoughts, and feelings. Just paying attention, becoming more familiar and intimate with yourself, much like the activity of the first bricklayer.

Like the second bricklayer, meditation can also be done with a specific intention or goal in mind: to reduce stress, to build focus and perspective, or as the basis for improving emotional intelligence. As my coteacher said, bringing your attention back to your breath, again and again, is much like building muscles in the gym; you train the mind to become more focused. We can also practice with a kind of open awareness, not focusing on any one object, as a way of building a more flexible mind.

Finally, meditation can be a kind of sacred act, like the third bricklayer. As Dogen describes: We take the backward step, adopt a posture of "repose and bliss," without trying to perform an activity called meditation. This might be described as creating meaning, but I think it is that and much more than that. This approach to meditation invites an experience outside of our usual understanding — as Dogen says elsewhere: "Drop away body and mind and your original face will be manifest." In this sense, practicing meditation becomes an expression of our most healthy, whole "original" self.

Meditation practice is each and all of these things.

MEDITATION FAQ

Here are answers to some of the most frequently asked questions I receive about meditation:

How often should I meditate?

Having a daily meditation practice is optimal. A few times a week or weekly is better than not having a practice.

How long should each meditation session be?

I like to sit for twenty to thirty minutes. On occasion I like to do longer sittings. Whatever you can manage is good. I know many people who sit for a few minutes each day. Regularity counts for more than the length of each session. Occasionally going on retreats with a group — for a half or full day, or for several days — can be a terrific way to deepen your practice.

I like to run, swim, or go for walks.
Is that the same as meditation?

Physical activity is essential for health and well-being and may provide many of the benefits of meditation. There is also something distinctive about just sitting without any of the activity or stimulation of exercise.

Walking Meditation

I think of the practice of walking meditation not as a substitute for the practice of sitting meditation but as an important complementary activity. Like mindful listening, it is a way of taking meditation into movement.

I generally teach three types of walking meditation. First is the slowest and most formal kind, and it is sometimes done in Zen centers between periods of sitting meditation. Begin by standing and bringing full attention to your body and mind. Then, as you exhale, take half a step. As you step, be aware that you are raising one foot off the ground, lifting it in the air, and then placing it on the ground. Bring awareness to your body as you complete the step. Once your foot is on the ground, inhale and gently shift your weight forward. With the next exhale, take another half step and repeat the process. This practice synchronizes walking with breathing. Do this for five to ten minutes each day, or whenever possible, as part of your routine.

Just as in sitting meditation, sometimes you focus on your breath and body. Other times, you can open your awareness to your senses, including anything in your environment, any sounds, anything you might be feeling. As thoughts arise, notice them as well, and bring your attention back to your body and breath as you step.

The next style of walking meditation is somewhat less formal. In this type, walk slowly and mindfully to a predetermined spot about twenty or thirty feet away. When you reach that spot, stop, turn around, and walk back.

The third kind of walking meditation is what I call stealth meditation. In this method, you meditate while walking during the course of a regular day and while walking normally. Perhaps you are walking to or from the restroom, to your car or a meeting, or along a path in nature. Just walking. But you know that you are doing walking meditation — you are more focused, present, and aware.

Explore and experiment with each of these three types.

Journal Writing

Writing in a journal can provide an experience and benefits similar to meditation practice: While sitting quietly and bringing attention to body, mind, breath, and feelings, you write. Many studies have demonstrated the effectiveness of journal writing in developing self-awareness, reducing stress, and cultivating well-being. Like meditation, I suggest journaling on a regular basis. Try to do so a few minutes a day or more.

There are many kinds of journal writing. Most often, I teach free writing, which mirrors sitting meditation. Start with a prompt and begin writing, without planning or editing, much like the flow of consciousness that you may experience during sitting meditation.

TRY THIS: Get pencil and paper or use your computer. Using one of the prompts below, start writing and continue writing, without editing or thinking too much, for two minutes. Set a timer if you like, or have a clock or watch you can see. Write whatever the prompt makes you think of. Just see what emerges. No one else will read what you have written. You might be surprised. The only rule is to keep the pen or keys moving. If you can't think of what to say, write, "I have nothing to say..." until something else comes to you.

Here are several prompts to choose from. Use these to inspire your own.

- My challenges are...
- What annoys me is...
- What brings me alive is...
- Love is...
- What I'm feeling right now is...
- What surprises me about my life right now is...

INTEGRATED PRACTICE: AN APPROPRIATE RESPONSE

The Zen tradition has a dialogue in which a student asks the teacher, "What is the teaching of an entire lifetime?" The teacher answers, "An appropriate response."

How simple. How elegant. The teaching of an entire lifetime can be captured in the way you respond. Integrated practice is how we bring mindfulness practice into daily life, and it is defined by how we respond in any moment.

How do *you* respond to the events, surprises, opportunities, and problems in your life? Effectively, wisely, skillfully, reactively, tenderly, fiercely? This Zen dialogue says, in essence, that the most important teaching in life is to respond in the most appropriate way to each and every situation. But doing that is challenging in the midst of our busy lives and everyday concerns, and what defines "an appropriate response" to begin with? One guideline for an appropriate response is to ask: What response is most likely to have the best possible outcome for all involved?

The appropriate response would meet each circumstance in the "best" way, the one that's most authentic, alive, skillful, effective, wise, courageous, and compassionate. As much as possible, it would align with our values and deepest intentions, so perhaps it is the most heartfelt, vulnerable, open, and transparent response. The appropriate response may be anger or curiosity. It may be the most considered or the most spontaneous response. It might be a heartfelt apology for a mistake, for less-than-stellar behavior, or for unintentionally causing someone pain. It might be to celebrate an achievement. It might be to put aside everything else to experience and express the joy of being alive.

Or, to put this differently, one way you know that you are "doing the work" is when you notice you are responding more appropriately. This means not only meditating as a dedicated practice but also integrating mindfulness into the ways you live your daily life — by cultivating awareness, aliveness, curiosity, presence, and integrity into your work and relationships. In this sense, doing the work is an outlook, an attitude, and an intention as well as the specific actions you take. If dedicated practice represents regular activities you do to become more aware, integrated practice represents your intention and attempt to be mindful at all times — or as often as you can.

The real question is: Why don't we respond appropriately all the time? What keeps us from being mindful? Here are four common obstacles:

We lack awareness of others or the situation.
We feel judgmental and self-critical.
We become afraid and react without thinking.
We fear change.

The rest of this chapter will explore how to work with those obstacles with the following four core integrated practices. These are examples of what it means to "do the work," and all will be explored further in the rest of this book. They are as follows:

Listen openly.
Prioritize self-compassion.
Cultivate emotional awareness.
Seek alignment.

TO CULTIVATE AWARENESS, LISTEN OPENLY

How you show up and respond in any situation depends on the quality of your listening. Listening to others is particularly important for leaders, since creating agreement and a shared sense of purpose are key, which means cultivating trust through awareness of each individual's needs, desires, and strengths. The leader's role is also to see the big picture, the larger context, but we can't do that alone, from our limited perspective.

Real listening means letting go of being right, which requires a paradoxical blend of confidence and humility.

Otto Scharmer, a senior lecturer at MIT and author of *Leading from the Emerging Future*, describes four levels of listening.

1. **DISTRACTED LISTENING** — a very common form of listening. Instead of really listening, we are thinking of what we are going to say or how someone's words are impacting us.
2. **LISTENING FOR FACTS** — listening to the content of what is being said.
3. **EMPATHIC LISTENING** — listening for feelings. Not only paying attention to content but noticing what feelings are being expressed.
4. **GENERATIVE LISTENING** — listening with curiosity and openness. Listening underneath and in between the words and feelings for clues as to what the speaker may be implying or moving toward. This form of listening sometimes arises as a feeling, image, or intuition. It is a way of helping another person see more clearly; it is not advice giving or problem solving.

Listening may be one of the most underappreciated activities and skills, not only for leaders, but for everyone. It is central to all our relationships, and yet it generally receives surprisingly little attention. In many of the trainings I've led, regardless of the industry, position, or culture of the participants, I find that people are stunned to discover the power of listening. And they are surprised to discover how rarely they truly listen — listen without interrupting, without planning the "right" or any response, just being fully present, without any agenda. Listening to another person can take us out of the narrow, self-centered world that we often unknowingly create and open us to another person's experience. This can shift our experience of ourselves and foster a connection with another person that fulfills the empathic ape's need and longing for trust and openness.

TRY THIS: Experiment with these four levels of listening:

- Notice when you are not listening and when listening for facts.
- Experiment with empathic listening. How do you know what someone else is feeling? With a close friend or partner, you might explore asking what they are feeling as they are speaking.
- Explore generative listening. Coaches, consultants, and medical professionals do this regularly. Open yourself to listening between the lines, using your intuition. After voicing a feeling, image, or opening that you see, explore how this resonates with the person you are listening to.

TO AVOID JUDGMENT, PRIORITIZE SELF-COMPASSION

I once led a two-day mindfulness and emotional intelligence training for a group of eighty participants, business leaders, and managers from around the world. At the end of the training, a CEO of a growing start-up company approached me to let me know how meaningful and useful the training had been. Then he added, "Mindfulness practice helped me be somewhat less self-critical and self-judgmental. If that was the only outcome, for most of the people in the room, the training would have been a huge success."

Many people, especially leaders, believe that they need to be self-critical and tough with themselves in order to be motivated and successful. When faced with a problem, or with failure, we often feel that the best response is judgment and punishment directed at ourselves. I find, however, that the opposite is often more effective and successful. This is where the empathic ape comes in. If the nervous ape alerts us to threats, and the imaginative ape helps us evaluate them, the empathic ape can guide us to what is always our best response: compassion, whether in regard to others or ourselves.

Why is it that compassion, acceptance, and nonjudgment are so hard? I think there are many different reasons, some subtle and some just bad habits. Kristin Neff is one of the world's leading researchers on the topic of self-compassion. Here are some of the most common challenges or fears she has discovered in her research:

- **FEAR OF PASSIVITY:** This is the misconception that accepting ourselves and being kind to ourselves is a form of avoidance and will lead to greater passivity, thus taking the edge off of ambition and driving change. I've heard people say that if they weren't tough and critical, they would not be as productive. I sometimes suggest to my executive coaching clients that they test this assumption and experiment with being kind to themselves for one week, then notice if it negatively impacts their productivity. (They nearly always discover an increase in productivity and a decrease in stress.)

- **APATHY OF ETHICS:** Sometimes we fear that we will become less attentive to ethical concerns, to issues of right and wrong and their consequences.
- **NO MOTIVATION TO CHANGE:** By accepting ourselves, we think we will be less motivated and less able to make important changes.
- **REDUCTION OF EFFORT:** This is the mistaken idea that acceptance will lead to less effort to make changes or to meet goals.

However, research shows that in all of these dimensions, an attitude of acceptance is actually constructive. A series of studies conducted by Juliana Breines and Serena Chen evaluated how participants responded to setbacks, mistakes, and their own weaknesses. The participants were divided into three groups: (1) a control group that had no intervention, (2) a "self-esteem" group that was asked to journal about positive characteristics about themselves, and (3) a "self-compassion" group that was asked to journal about themselves and their challenges from a perspective of understanding, acceptance, and self-compassion.

The researchers measured these four different outcomes: (1) Growth mindset (a belief in the possibility of change), (2) motivation to make amends after an ethical transgression, (3) motivation to improve on a weakness, and (4) effort to improve; in this case, students' time spent studying more after performing poorly on a test.

Compared to the control group and the self-esteem group, the self-compassion group scored higher on all four dimensions. The results were that those in the self-compassion group were more likely to have a growth mindset, more likely to want to fix a past ethical transgression, had more motivation to improve, and spent more effort improving. The takeaway from this study is that self-compassion is a more effective way to meet our challenges than doing nothing (of course), *and* it's more effective than trying to "boost our self-esteem" (another common strategy) by skipping over the difficulty and emphasizing a positive self-image.

Here's what the authors concluded: "Self-compassion may increase self-improvement motivation given that it encourages people to confront their mistakes and weaknesses without either self-deprecation or defensive self-enhancement."

To be able to face difficulties "without either self-deprecation or defensive self-enhancement" also enables sustainable self-confidence — as the research showed, the self-compassion group tended to have more confidence in their ability to grow and to be more interested in spending time with people they looked up to.

TRY THIS: Take six minutes to write a letter to yourself, as if from the perspective of someone who knows you well, understands you, and wants the best for you. What would he or she say about the challenges and opportunities you are facing?

TO AVOID REACTIVITY, CULTIVATE EMOTIONAL AWARENESS

As I describe in practice 1, humans did not evolve to respond wisely or appropriately; we evolved to avoid threats, so that we would survive and thus pass on our genes. The nervous ape scans for threats constantly, externally and internally, and it developed three primary responses to any potential danger: fight, flight, or freeze. In an emergency, in any extreme or life-threatening situation, these are very effective, appropriate responses.

For instance, I was hiking once in the hills in the Marin Headlands. As I stepped, my right foot touched what my body perceived was a snake. Instantly, I felt the chemistry in my stomach and chest shift, and I jumped in alarm! Then, in the next instant, I saw that the snake was actually a stick. The alarm bells stopped, my flight response eased, and very quickly, my body's chemistry shifted back to its resting state. On another occasion, I was hiking in the same place when I spotted a mountain lion crossing the trail ahead of me and moving into a crouching position, as though it was hunting. Again, I experienced alarm; my body systems shifted instantly. I was particularly aware of the lion's hunting posture, since I thought that it might be hunting me. I made myself appear as large as possible, slowly backed away, and took a different route to my car.

In both cases, I had an appropriate response! In the first incident, the response was unwarranted, but my body reacted correctly to the threat it perceived: a snake. If I'd hesitated to wonder, "Wait, is this really a snake?" it could have proved fatal. The nervous ape survives by overreacting to all potential threats and living to laugh about it.

When threatened, our bodies are amazing and effective in shutting down the parasympathetic nervous system and shifting into survival mode. The amygdala, the alarm bell of the brain, takes over. When threatened, the appropriate response that is built into our body chemistry is to fight, flee, or freeze — responses that have the highest likelihood of survival. However, most physical threats, and most perceived threats, are not genuinely life-endangering. If we spent our life jumping at sticks, we would not be practicing the most skilled, appropriate response. Nor does it help us to engage in fight, flight, or freeze when receiving a challenging email from a boss, when being cut off by another car on the highway, or when losing an important customer.

To one degree or another, all of the seven practices help cultivate emotional awareness, since that is the essence of mindfulness. But the most difficult situation in which to apply mindfulness is when we are triggered, when we react instinctively out of fear, without thinking. Emotional triggers can be subtle or not so subtle — we may be triggered from an actual threat or only a perceived threat. If we perceive anger in someone's voice or an email, we may feel triggered to avoid that person, shout back, or shut down. It doesn't much matter whether the anger we perceive is real and genuine (a hunting lion) or illusory and mistaken (a harmless stick). We may not be able to stop our initial emotional response, but mindfulness helps us respond appropriately in the next moment, with awareness. Otherwise, we might, or even likely will, make things worse.

For instance, if another driver cuts us off, and we feel that spike of road rage, do we chase that driver down, shouting, and risk causing the very accident that triggered our fear? Do we break the stick to pieces because we thought for a moment it would hurt us?

Emotional awareness allows us to pause before responding, assess the situation and our feelings, and then act in the most effective way.

TRY THIS: Whenever you are emotionally triggered, stop. Just notice. Be curious. Be cautious about blaming or making assumptions about another person's motivations. As other practices will guide you: Don't presume to know, and connect to your own and the other person's emotions.

When the moment passes, ask yourself: In what way does this emotion feel familiar? Is there a pattern I can learn from? How do you respond to change, to difficulty, to success, to failure? How do you respond when you feel certain or when you are unsure? How do you respond when angry or when experiencing a significant loss? Do you tend to seek, avoid, or ignore conflict?

Then ask: Right now and in the future, what response might have the best possible outcome for all?

TO AVOID FEAR OF CHANGE, SEEK ALIGNMENT

When I first began teaching mindfulness and emotional intelligence in the business world, I thought that, as employees developed greater self-awareness and emotional awareness, they would become happier, more likely to enjoy their work, and more likely to remain longer with their company. Much of the time, for many employees, this is true: The benefits of mindfulness can lead to greater productivity, leadership skills, well-being, and satisfaction in their current job.

However, for some people, mindfulness makes them aware of a significant lack of alignment between their values and their work. They discover that either the culture of their workplace doesn't fit or the work they are doing is not what is most suited to them. Following mindfulness trainings, I've noticed that people sometimes change roles within their companies or even leave their companies to pursue work that is more meaningful, more in alignment with their values and needs.

Mindfulness practice doesn't cause people to become

dissatisfied. Rather, it helps people see their "ground truth" and "creative gaps" more clearly. Sometimes we ignore or deny our ground truth because we fear change, particularly when it leads into unknown territory. So we hesitate, defer, rationalize not changing, or talk ourselves out of our dissatisfactions. But once we become self-aware of how we truly feel, the appropriate response is to seek alignment, to change. In fact, that's one way to evaluate what's an appropriate response: it is an action that creates alignment with what's most important.

When I look at the major transitions in my life, they generally were precipitated by change or growth in my own awareness that led me to recognize a lack of alignment between what was important to me and what I was doing. While an undergraduate student at Rutgers, as my interest and passion in meditation and mindfulness grew, I needed to leave Rutgers in order to pursue those interests. After ten years of living at the San Francisco Zen Center, the most important thing for me became integrating mindfulness practice with work practice in a more conventional setting, outside of the Zen Center. Seeking alignment, I left the monastery and went to business school and began working in the business world.

Life is always changing, we are always changing, and so we are always moving in and out of alignment. When we pay attention, we are nearly always in some kind of transition. Everyone and everything is dynamic, shifting, evolving. We need to ask ourselves regularly: What is most important right now, and is what I'm doing in alignment with that?

TRY THIS: To help shed some light on alignment, write for seven minutes on this topic: *In what ways are my work and life* *aligned with what is most important to me? In what ways am I not in alignment? What actions might I take to be more aligned?*

THE FULL CATASTROPHE

In the midst of our full catastrophe — of work, marriage, children, parents, everything — remaining mindful and intuiting the appropriate response in each moment is hard. Being a mindful leader can mean making tough decisions or listening to others and deferring to their wishes. It can mean guiding the group or simply holding space. As an example of what this looks like in real life, here is a story of my own journey, when I aspired to take care of my mother and to practice mindfulness during a most difficult time.

When my mother was living in Boca Raton, Florida, she was diagnosed with a brain tumor. Many events and a variety of responses unfolded following this diagnosis. At the time, I was living north of San Francisco, with my wife and two young children. I was still CEO of Brush Dance, and much of my energy was focused on running this small, quickly growing business. In response to my mother's illness, in order to better take care of her, my wife and I invited her to move from Florida to our home in Northern California. This meant selling her home in Florida and facing what would most likely be the final chapter in her life. My mother loved her home and her community in Boca Raton, where she had lived for seventeen years.

Still, she agreed to come live with us. Within weeks, she sold or gave away her car, furniture, and most everything that she owned and arrived at my family's home. None of us knew what the timeframe would be for this new living arrangement. Doctors had advised us that she might live for months or possibly for years. I think we all recognized that this would be challenging, involving stress and adjustments for everyone, but there was no question that the most important thing was for my mother to spend her remaining time with us.

During the next months, we experienced many wonderful and beautiful times of intimacy and connection. My children, then twelve and seven, loved having their grandmother so close and responded by doing what they could to take care of her. Nevertheless, I remember coming home from work one day during a lunch break, on a day when my schedule was particularly packed, to take my mother to a doctor's appointment. She had agreed to be dressed and ready when I arrived, but when I got home, I found her just getting out of her nightgown. I felt triggered and reacted impatiently in a mix of frustration, irritation, and anger. Then, as I looked more closely, I could see my mother struggling to put her clothing on. She was in pain, trying her best. I was not responding as I aspired to, with compassion. I'd come home to help take care of her, and I noticed a gaping gulf between my reaction and my deeper intentions. I managed to pause and catch myself. *Lesser, what are you doing?* I asked myself, feeling ashamed. I relaxed and dropped my story — my idea that I had important work-related tasks I needed to hurry back to. I shifted, became more fully present and responsive, and helped my mother get dressed. I went from feeling irritable, frustrated, and disconnected to feeling tender, loving, and compassionate. I called my office and had others cover for me.

A few weeks later, at another doctor's appointment, it was discovered that my mother had a severe lung infection. After examining her, the doctor took me aside to inform me that she probably would not live more than a few days. He explained that one option was to admit her to the hospital and explore a variety of invasive, emergency procedures, but at best these might extend her life by a few days or weeks. I asked him, "If she were your mother, what would you do?" He responded, "I would take her home and make her comfortable."

However, this was not my decision to make. The doctor and I went to speak with my mother. We told her about her condition and that she probably didn't have long to live. I told her everything: what her options were and how the doctor had responded to my question. She responded with a beautiful mix of sadness, love, satisfaction, and resignation. "Okay, let's go home" she said. "I've lived a good and long life. I'm ready." I was amazed by my mother's response, by her ability to face and completely accept her situation with such courage and grace. We hugged, cried, and drove home.

It was self-evident to me and my wife that we should give my mother our bedroom, which was the quietest, most protected part of our home. I don't remember there being much discussion. My mother's response: She refused our offer and headed directly for the most central and active part of the house, our living room, and lay down on the couch. That was the spot she wanted to be: not isolated, but completely accessible to our entire family, right in the midst of the daily activity. I was surprised by her request, but I agreed without hesitating. I respected her sense of where she wanted to spend the last few days of her life.

The next day, she was lying on our couch, clearly quite weak. I decided to make her a fruit smoothie, which I knew was one of her favorite foods. As I handed her a large, full glass with a straw to make it easier for her to drink, she asked, "What are you doing? I'm trying to die and you are making me a fruit smoothie." I responded, "It's fine with me if you die, Mom. I just want you to die healthy." We both laughed and cried.

A few days later she became weaker, quieter, and calmer. Late at night, my wife and I sat next to her as she was lying down on our living room couch. We began to notice her breath becoming slower and more full. We both began to breathe with her. And then there was that moment: a long, slow exhale, with no inhale following. We sat with a great sense of stillness, sadness, and letting go.

DO THE WORK

KEY PRACTICES

- Implement or continue dedicated mindfulness practices: Create a regular routine of meditation, walking meditation, and journal writing, in any combination.
- Implement or continue an integrated mindfulness practice. Ask, "What is the appropriate response?"
- Listen for facts and for feelings, and practice generative listening.
- Practice self-compassion; experiment with kindness.
- Whenever you feel triggered or reactive, pause, evaluate the appropriate response, and cultivate emotional awareness.
- Whenever you fear change, identify your ground truth or creative gaps, and act to seek alignment.

PRACTICE 3

DON'T BE AN EXPERT

The Scientific Revolution has not been a revolution of knowledge. It has been above all a revolution of ignorance. The great discovery that launched the Scientific Revolution was the discovery that humans do not know the answers to their most important questions.

— YUVAL NOAH HARARI, *Sapiens: A Brief History of Humankind*

The word *mindfulness* is a translation of the Pali word *sati*. It literally means "to remember" — to remember that you are here, awake, alive, free. To remember where you came from, where you are going, and where you are right now. To remember the pain and possibility of being human. To remember to shift from autopilot to being aware. To remember to bring attention to the minute details and the immeasurable immensity of being alive. To remember to see, hear, feel, taste, and touch as though for the first time and as though your time on earth were limited, which it is. To remember to appreciate your body, mind, and heart. To remember to notice where you are holding back and to imagine what your life would be like if you were not holding back at all. To remember the amazing, mysterious, paradoxical nature of your life, that you were born and that you will die.

What gets in the way of remembering? Fears, habits, distractions, lust, aversion, restlessness, and more. These are all challenges for anyone, including leaders. One particular hindrance to remembering that stands out in the realm of mindful leadership is thinking we're right. Thinking there is a correct answer and we know it.

Whenever I teach mindfulness and meditation in the corporate world — to health care professionals, to social entrepreneurs, to engineers, managers, and executives at Google, Disney, or SAP — I'm struck by how quickly and strongly the desire arises to compete, to excel, to be the best meditator. During our initial meditation together, I often see people's effort — extra, unnecessary effort — expressed via a tightening and tensing of shoulders, jaws, and facial muscles. Afterward, as participants ask questions about the practice of meditation, two underlying concerns quickly surface: (1) Am I doing it wrong? And (2) are others doing it better?

When I answer these concerns by suggesting that an important element of mindfulness meditation practice is dropping our usual judgments about right and wrong, I often see somewhat curious looks as well as a sense of relief on people's faces. There is no doing meditation wrong or doing it right. I generally propose that people give up trying to be the best meditators. When it comes to the practices of mindfulness and meditation, a central instruction is: Don't be an expert.

Trying to be an expert is misleading, irrelevant, and even counterproductive when it comes to mindfulness. In fact, a key benefit of mindfulness meditation is that it helps us directly experience and understand that our pictures, stories, and mental models of the world are incomplete, often biased, and at times misguided. Training in mindfulness meditation means letting go of striving for success and letting go of fearing failure. This realization and understanding allows us to be more open, curious, and flexible — about our own thinking, feelings, and ideas as well as about the thinking, feelings, and ideas of others. This can transform the quality of how we listen to ourselves and to others and allow for greater understanding and connection.

When I first present practice 3, "Don't be an expert," to leaders and to people in the business world, I am often met with skeptical looks, shaking heads, and responses like, "Why would I do that? In my company, I would be ridiculed, or even crushed, for not being an expert or for not using my expertise."

That might be true. In leadership and in business, being an expert is a highly valued and rewarded position. We need experts, and in truth, we usually spend our lives working hard to become expert in all our roles and functions — as parents, spouses, teachers, leaders, workers, students, and so on. Experts get the big salaries and bonuses, the straight As, the sought-after promotion, and failures are shown the door. Or so it seems.

But there are times to use your expertise and strive for excellence and times when those things get in the way, when they blind us rather than help us see the ground truth and what's most important. Paradoxically, if we approach mindfulness like a beginner and give up the need to be an expert, if we relax the need to feel safe, right, and important, this can bolster our confidence, flexibility, and effectiveness. This is true when it comes to mindfulness as well as for leadership, healthy relationships, and enjoying and appreciating this human life. Curiosity, openness, and being aware of how much we don't know are considerably more effective strategies than attempting to become an expert and then having to prove or defend our expertise.

One of Shunryu Suzuki's statements sums up perfectly this approach: "The most important thing in our practice is to have right or perfect effort. Our effort in our practice should be directed from achievement to nonachievement."

The concept of "right or perfect effort" is somewhat paradoxical. It is the effort to not make any extra or unnecessary effort. Even more difficult to understand and embody is "nonachievement," especially in the context of work and leadership. A key to leadership success, presence, and satisfaction is letting go of our extra effort and unnecessary striving to achieve those results.

Mindfulness, by definition, is to experience our actual, direct, unfiltered experience and the full spectrum of our senses, thoughts, and intuitions. Mindfulness helps us acknowledge the beauty and mystery of our human life, as well as the inner critic, the judge, our feelings of shame, our fears and fantasies. Mindfulness includes cultivating attitudes of freshness, warmheartedness, and compassion. Mindfulness itself can be defined as not being an expert, which might be why Shunryu Suzuki refers to the practice as adopting "beginner's mind."

NERVOUS APES LOVE BEING EXPERTS

It's safer and easier to be an expert. The default mode of the nervous ape is to scan for threats, externally and internally. The questioning, critical mind of the nervous ape often asks: *How am I doing? Am I right or wrong? Am I doing well or badly? Am I protected or vulnerable?*

To not know when others know, to lack information, and to be seen as unsure is to be vulnerable. It risks someone smarter and more skilled coming along and taking what we want. It risks not recognizing a threat when one appears. As nervous apes, we seek to learn as quickly as possible, and we feel better when we're certain. Once we "know," we can relax a bit, since the world becomes more predictable. We don't have to work as hard to understand, and threats and opportunities are easier to spot.

The last thing a nervous ape wants is to go back to being a "beginner." It works hard to become an "expert," and that status further enhances and enables its continued success. This isn't just an issue of status, however, and of our reluctance to let go of it. The difficulty also has to do with our sense of survival and habituated modes of thinking. This affects everyone, whether we consider ourselves experts or not.

This practice isn't about renouncing one's experience and skills. Rather, it defines what I feel is a productive way to approach nearly any situation: that is, with an open mind, one free of preconceived notions, much like a student or beginner. The attitude of the expert is "I know." The attitude of the beginner is "I am curious and want to learn."

This can be a difficult attitude for the nervous ape to adopt, which is why we often struggle with it. And yet, doing so is useful and effective. Our relationship with our self is the basis for all our other relationships, and the practice of beginner's mind is foundational for learning and for personal growth and development. The practice of beginner's mind is cultivating a relationship of inquiry and openness with ourselves.

This is what mindfulness teaches: how to respond and engage with openness and curiosity, how to observe while suspending judgment. When we practice mindfulness, we neither agree with a thought or belief nor disagree and react with skepticism. We adopt an attitude of inquiry that neither confirms nor rejects what we find. Either response — whether confirming what already aligns with our beliefs or pushing away what doesn't align — is often the reflexive mental habit of the nervous ape. It's generally a form of autopilot. It's what develops once we believe in our own proficiency and expertise.

All seven practices are about noticing and transforming our habit mind, our autopilot, our asleep mind — the mind that narrows awareness and attention. Beginner's mind doesn't require adding anything; rather, it undoes assumptions and habits. In fact, each activity *is* new and fresh; each moment *is* alive. We don't create this; we can only notice it. The term *beginner's mind* simply describes our ability to experience what actually is.

EMBRACE FAILURE

Most models of leadership emphasize knowing and understanding, making decisions based on that knowledge, and persuading others that we know what to do. Yet mindfulness asks us not to act in these ways, which can make us feel extremely vulnerable, since we've evolved and learned to expect that, as leaders, this equals failure.

Thus, the starting point with this practice is to be less reactive. We aim to shift our mental framework away from reactiveness and protection and toward greater responsiveness. One great way to do this is to embrace failure, to practice and embody the reality that we can fail, survive, and learn. This was one of the first exercises I learned during an introduction to improv class I once attended at Bay Area Theatre Sports (BATS) in Fort Mason, San Francisco. Zoe Galvez, my teacher, instructed the class of sixteen participants to throw our arms into the air, smile broadly, and loudly proclaim, "I failed!" Then again, "I failed!" And a third time, this time with heart, "I failed!"

Announcing failure can be great fun and strangely liberating. Letting go of the fear of failure, even celebrating failure, was an important basis to practicing improvisational theater. Improv theater always risks failure, and every improv actor fails, time and time again, and yet they can't let failure stop the show. Learning improv was an experimental and safe space to take risks and not to worry about winning or losing, or looking good or bad, or trying to do it right.

I began taking improv classes at BATS to help me be less terrified when speaking in front of audiences. I used to have nightmares about speaking to an audience, without a written script and not knowing what to say. Improv classes helped a lot. Cultivating this attitude, an attitude of beginner's mind, has supported me to feel more relaxed and confident, right in the midst of my anxiety. Since then, I have learned and grown. For many years, I have led trainings with a wide range of groups. I have developed a good deal of experience and confidence in public speaking, but I still have to remind myself to avoid the nervous ape's impulse to consider myself either a failure or "the expert."

I sometimes do this "I failed" exercise in my mindful leadership workshops, and at times I have incorporated it into the Search Inside Yourself program — as a way of cutting through our usual beliefs and attachments to success and failure. In one of my leadership workshops, a forty-five-year-old Austrian psychiatrist began to weep after participating in this exercise. He said he had never done anything like this. Since birth he felt that he was trained only to succeed. He only got the best grades, went to the best schools, and became a successful doctor. He felt moved and freed in this short moment of letting go of trying so hard to be an expert.

This is an easy practice to do on your own. Experiment with shifting your attitude to accepting failure. There are many opportunities, small and large, throughout an average day, such as any time you are late (I failed!), forget someone's name (I failed!), spill something (I failed!), make a mistake (I failed!), and so on. First, notice your habitual response to failure. If you are like me, you may tighten or constrict and feel annoyed, impatient, or angry. Instead of tightening and constricting, see if you can shift your reaction: Acknowledge that an expectation was not met and think, "Isn't that interesting." Then, play the "I failed" game. Say to yourself or out loud to someone else: "I failed!" As you do, smile like you mean it. And, importantly, if you do tighten, try just noticing that, instead of tightening about your tightening.

SEE THROUGH FRESH EYES: THIS TIME IS THE FIRST TIME

Every day, I see or hear something
that more or less
kills me with delight.

— Mary Oliver

Do you remember the first time that you rode a bicycle, drove a car, used a new software program, or had your first kiss? Remember that feeling of awkwardness and newness, the sense of excitement, learning, and richness in that experience?

Right now, do you notice that you are breathing? Of course you are breathing, and you've been breathing since the moment you were born, but have you considered that this particular breath is new, has never happened before, and won't happen again, ever? It is easy to forget this reality, to take it for granted. We have so many more important things to do and consider. But try pausing right now: Be curious about this breath, and then the next breath. The same is true for everything we do — riding a bike, driving a car, learning new software, kissing. Everything has a first time, and yet every experience is different, and unique, each and every time thereafter.

Usually, that's not how we experience it. Once we do something a few times, or dozens or thousands of times, it becomes familiar. Once something is familiar, we stop paying as much attention to it. Many things we stop paying attention to completely. Like breathing. Or walking. Walking is a big deal when we are babies trying to get places. Watching a young baby discover how to walk can be inspiring: watching the whole process of standing, stepping once, holding on for balance, experimenting, falling and failing over and over, and finally putting it all together. Then, once you are a walking expert, and for as long as you walk without pain or difficulty, you most likely pay very little or no attention to the act of walking.

Personally, I've had two hip replacement surgeries in recent years. (Yes, I am a bionic man.) Walking without pain is something I no longer take for granted, at least most of the time. Sometimes I forget, perhaps because I am focusing on a conversation or another activity while walking. Other times I pause to remember: *Oh, this used to be painful, so painful that I was unable to walk very far.* In these moments of awareness, I feel grateful: It's amazing to have two titanium hips. I appreciate the researchers and scientists who introduced these devices and the medical advances, the breakthroughs, required to develop this technology. I appreciate my surgeon, along with my wife and family for caring for me after the surgery.

Then, of course, I go back to walking, and I forget. Our tendency is to forget, to lose interest in whatever we are doing, particularly whatever comes easily or is repeated often. As we become more skilled, and do certain things over and over, we tend to take these activities for granted. This has advantages. We don't need to think about breathing, walking, thinking, speaking, or seeing. These familiar activities require so little attention they become automatic.

Unfortunately, this habituation, this sense of expertise, of taking things for granted, can apply to how we think about ourselves, our relationships, and the world. Most of our activities may feel automatic. No part of our life is immune. The practice "Don't be an expert" means reducing the filters of expectation and habituation, which get in the way of seeing how alive and rich our sensations are, how alive and rich each moment is.

TRY THIS: Hold up your right hand with your palm facing you. Just take a few moments to look, to see, to notice. See if you can look without naming, without words, without judgment. Shift your attitude from achievement — such as wanting to do this exercise well — and let go of seeking or grasping at a result. What do you see and feel? This hand: Is it you, or only part of you? Consider that you didn't make this hand, which is more complex than anything a human being can make. Try moving your fingers: These small muscle movements are driven by more than two hundred thousand neurons. Notice the shapes of each part of your hand without using the part's name. Notice the lines in the skin. As you do this, notice that you are breathing. Notice if, or when, your thinking mind asserts itself — thoughts of judgment (*I didn't know my fingers were so fat!*) or self-consciousness (*Why am I doing this strange exercise?*). Bring your attention back to your hand, and stay with this experiment for a few moments longer than you feel you should. What else do you notice? About your thoughts and your breathing? What do you notice about your hand? Have you ever spent time like this before, getting to know the body that is yourself?

For the rest of the day or week, or whenever you think of it, practice looking at everything with fresh eyes: at yourself, at the people you live and work with, at the world. Step back and remove, release, or reduce what you already know. Instead, see and listen with a sense of wonder and curiosity.

Another excellent way to experience this is to practice walking meditation (see pages 65–66). Explore walking with a childlike quality, as though doing it for the first time, and appreciate what a miracle it is. Bring mindfulness to walking whenever you think of it and see what happens.

BE HERE WHEN? REDUCE MIND WANDERING

Some psychological research estimates that 10 percent of our actions are conscious, and 90 percent are unconscious. That is, thinking, feeling, judgment, and actions are driven by automated, nonconscious activities. This automation process is said to have a neural basis. The activity of one of the oldest, most primal parts of the brain, the basal ganglia, transforms repeated conscious actions until they become habitual patterns.

Apparently, such automated processing doesn't necessarily free us to think deep, satisfying thoughts. Other studies have shown that most people experience mind wandering — that is, they are not focused on what they are actually doing — 47 percent of the time. Plus, this mind wandering is associated with anxiety that fosters unhappiness. For example, here is an abstract summary of a scientific paper by Justin Brewer, director of research at the University of Massachusetts Medical School.

> The default mode is mind wandering, not paying attention to what you are doing. Mind wandering is correlated with unhappiness in the brain. Mind wandering was shown to be deactivated in the brain via mindfulness meditation. Experienced meditators showed greater awareness and cognitive control, as measured by regions in the brain.

Or, to use this book's analogy, we might say: Nervous apes are not happy apes. Nor are imaginative or empathic apes. Our minds are constantly wandering in the same habitual ruts, focusing on uncertainty, anxiety, and "what ifs." Our minds wander in the past and in the future, chewing old wounds and conflicts, and anticipating known threats, and if we focus on the present, it's to defend ourselves.

Yet mindfulness meditation helps shift this. By practicing focused awareness and open-ended awareness, we learn to let go of habitual thinking and negative mind wandering. In a way, you might call open-ended awareness a type of positive mind wandering. This is what mindful walking cultivates. Of course, I think everyone experiences this sometimes, perhaps unexpectedly, such as while out in nature or while showering: New insights emerge, without any agenda to solve certain problems. This kind of positive mind wandering is free of worry or rumination, free of to-do lists, and free of concerns about time and place. These are the moments when we see the world and ourselves with fresh eyes.

TRY THIS: Everyone's mind wanders sometimes. Explore, be curious, and notice your own mind wandering. If you notice your mind is wandering, bring attention to it, without judging or trying to become an expert. Even for a few minutes each day, ask: *Am I focused and aware of what I'm doing? Am I consciously opening my awareness? Or am I ruminating about the past or worrying about the future?* Just notice.

EXPERIENCE FIRST, TELL STORIES LATER

Daniel Kahneman, a Nobel Prize–winning economist and psychology professor, describes people as having two distinct selves: the experiencing self and the remembering or narrative self. The experiencing self lives in the moment and in the world of sensations. The narrative self creates stories to make sense of what is experienced. Being an expert is a story, and if our focus is using, displaying, or confirming our expertise, then we are less focused on what's actually happening in the moment.

Kahneman has conducted a variety of fascinating experiments to clarify the distinction between these two selves as well as to demonstrate conflicts between these parts of us, especially when it comes to the perception of time and how our remembered selves are influenced by what he describes as the peaks and ends of an experience or event. For example, our memory of a vacation may be colored by one or two moments that stand out as strongly positive or negative peaks, as well as by our experience of the last part of the vacation. In *Thinking, Fast and Slow,* Kahneman writes:

> The two selves are the experiencing self, which does the living, and the remembering self, which keeps score and makes the choices.... We should not forget, however, that the perspective of the remembering self is not always correct.... The remembering self's neglect of

> duration, its exaggerated emphasis on peaks and ends, and its susceptibility to hindsight combine to yield distorted reflections of our actual experience.

Remembering and storytelling is the realm of the imaginative ape, who processes sensations and experiences and weaves a narrative that makes sense of what we call self — our identity, values, and needs — and puts them in the context of relationships, work, and life.

As Kahneman points out, the trouble is...these stories are often inaccurate. Not only is our personal perspective limited, so that we never see the whole picture, but even our perspective of our own experience and memories is often biased. As a matter of course, we choose only certain aspects of our experience as important and build a story out of those. In other words, we might assume that we are at least experts about our self, our history, and our identity, but Kahneman makes clear we should be skeptical of that claim as well.

TRY THIS: See if you can observe the distinction between your experiencing self and your narrative self. Play with noticing pure experience — in any moment, what do you see, hear, smell, taste, and touch? Then, pay attention to what you remember as important and how you create a narrative or a story that makes sense of yourself, others, and the world. What can you learn from this, by discerning what you experience from the story that you create about your experience?

LISTEN WITH OPEN EARS: DON'T BE A RELATIONSHIP EXPERT

For mindful leaders, the practice of not being an expert is particularly useful in relationships. Some of my favorite opening lines from a book are from *The Politics of Experience* by R. D. Laing:

> I cannot experience your experience
> You cannot experience my experience
> Therefore we are invisible to each other

Invisible is a strong word. I believe that, as empathic apes, we can sense, share, and convey feelings. But we are not mind readers. My takeaway from Laing is that we shouldn't assume we know someone else's experience. We are limited by our perspective and frequently wrong. Therefore, it is useful to practice being attentive and curious in order to increase our understanding of others. Usually, the more familiar we become with others, the more we assume we "know" them. We risk believing we are "relationship experts."

The practice of beginner's mind, of not assuming we know, is a way to build greater understanding and trust, especially when we have a disagreement or conflict with someone else. Listening is a key skill in creating that trust and connection.

In practice 1, I note that one of the three "jobs" of a leader is to listen (see pages 53–54), and in practice 2, I describe four levels of listening (see page 70). But what is the quality of your listening? That is the key question to ask whenever you are in conversation with someone. Are you listening to discover, to learn, and to expand your world? Or are you listening for your own benefit, through the filters of your needs and fears, or to confirm your own story, which reflects your need to be the expert?

In your conversations, explore listening with beginner's mind — without judgment and expectation. This is much like generative listening. Being willing to be surprised by what the other person is saying. We've been listening our entire lives, but how often are we really hearing what the other person is saying, feeling, meaning? How often do we seek to learn what is invisible to us?

What I think of as "filters" often clog our ears and distort what we hear, or what we understand someone to mean. These filters relate to the three apes: They might be the nervous ape's fears or perception of a threat. They might be the imaginative ape's story of our expertise, leadership, priorities, and goals, of what needs to be accomplished. They might be the empathic ape's assumptions and mistaken beliefs based on what we sense, feel, and see in the other.

To practice not being an expert in relationships, notice your filters. What attitudes, stories, fears, and desires get in the way of listening to and seeing someone else's experience? Practice cultivating being present for whatever is happening in this moment, with an attitude of curiosity and warmheartedness. When in doubt, ask for feedback from others. The nature of filters is that we don't notice them. Others or the world appear a certain way, and we think we are seeing what actually is, until someone points out our filters. Then we have a choice: Remove the filter and listen or look again, or create another filter by blaming others or circumstances or the world for not conforming to how we think, in our expertise, things should be.

Another good way to become self-aware of your filters, and to listen better, is to practice noticing the feelings of others. We tend to focus on our own feelings, and to react to what we feel, but if we reserve judgment, keep an open mind, and investigate the feelings of others, we might find unexpected solutions. In everyday life, experiment by being curious about how happy people are. Just notice, and listen.

TRY THIS: As an experiment, choose three people whom you know reasonably well and see regularly, either at work or at home, and rate what you believe their happiness level is on a scale of 1 to 10, with 10 being "very happy" and 1 being "very unhappy." Consider how you make this assessment — what is it based on? On their own words and body language, or on what you believe they feel or your own filters? See if you can notice your own judgments. Then for the next few days, pay attention to what these three people actually do and say, to how they behave. What do you learn?

FAILURE AND SUCCESS IN TOKYO

As is true in many areas of my life, it is easy to coach and teach others these practices. It is much more challenging to incorporate them into my own life. Here is one example of me being tested in the practice of beginner's mind and not being an expert.

When I first began my executive coaching and leadership consulting practice, I had a fair amount of confidence despite having little experience in this realm. One day I received a phone call asking if I would facilitate a three-day retreat in Tokyo for eight CEOs and their spouses from around the world. With both excitement and concern, I said yes. I was somewhat nervous, since I had never done anything like this, and I was excited to travel to Japan for the first time and to have the experience of leading a retreat.

Weeks before the retreat, I had a series of planning meetings with one of the group's members who was acting as the organizer. He communicated that the group was interested in experiencing a Zen style retreat. They wanted to be introduced to meditation and mindfulness practices; while they anticipated some discussion, the three days would be spent primarily in silence with a fair amount of meditation.

The sixteen participants, eight couples, were in their late fifties to midsixties and hailed from the United States, Australia, South America, and Europe. The men were all CEOs of midsized companies, and many were approaching retirement. I learned that this group had been meeting in different cities around the world once or twice a year for several years. They liked to begin their trips with a retreat, followed by touring whatever part of the world they were in for several days.

I thought the first day of the retreat went well. We sat two twenty-minute periods of meditation in the morning and in the afternoon. I organized several listening exercises and some journaling; free writing on several prompts that I gave them. Much of the day was spent in silence. I checked in with the organizer at the end of the day, who agreed things were off to a good start.

On the second day, we started with a short period of meditation, and then I suggested that we go around the table and each member of the group say one word to describe how they were feeling. The first person said, "Bored." The next person said, "Confused." And so it went counterclockwise around the room: "Curious." "Tired." "Unhappy." "Frustrated." A few positive and more neutral words were sprinkled among the negative ones.

I was stunned. Obviously, despite what I had thought, the retreat was not working for this group. I felt embarrassed and ashamed. I felt like a failure. Here I was in Tokyo, at the first business retreat I was leading, and people were not happy. As

I stood at the head of the long wooden conference table, the sixteen retreat participants looked at me, wondering what was going to happen next. I wanted to disappear, run away, or cry.

I took a few deeps breaths and noticed the mixture of feelings I was experiencing, the tightening of my jaw and chest. I knew this was a time to come forward with my best and highest self, to dig down deep to find as much equanimity, curiosity, and beginner's mind as I could muster. I looked at everyone and said, "Clearly, something is not working here. I apologize. I'm curious and interested — what is it that isn't working, and more importantly, what is it each of you wants from this time together? We have two more days scheduled. What would be most useful to each of you? Let's go around the circle and hear from everyone."

I was surprised to learn that these eight couples were eager to explore this time of transition in their lives. They were all in the midst of a major shift in their work and personal lives. For many, their children were no longer living with them. They expressed a mixture of fear and anticipation regarding retirement and the next stage of their lives. They wanted time to explore these issues with their partners and with the group.

I could have stuck to my agenda or attempted to maintain my role as an authority or expert. I don't think it would have worked out very well. Instead, I felt I needed to be transparent, present, curious, and open to learn what was actually happening and needed in this situation. I needed to let go of my assumptions, my needs, my fears, and my plan and listen to the participants.

I shifted the focus of the retreat toward an exploration of how they as individuals and as couples would engage with the next part of their lives. I got them into groups of threes to talk about their fears and their aspirations. Next, I asked them to go into separate spaces in the room as couples and had each of them answer the question, "Please tell me, how can I love you better?" During these encounters, a good deal of emotion and some tears were expressed. Now the retreat was much more aligned with their needs. When we came together as a group at the conclusion of the three-day retreat, and I again went around the table asking for a single word, people said: "Surprised." "Calm." "Community." "Hopeful."

The book *Be Here Now* by Ram Dass was published in 1971, when I was nineteen, and it had a major impact on me. It presented the possibility of finding a meaningful life by going beyond conventional ways of seeing ourselves and the world. I was introduced to the concept of not being an expert, of beginner's mind, through what Ram Dass called "the most exquisite paradox" — as soon as you give it all up, you can have it all. When you relax thinking that you already know, there are many more possibilities.

This practice is simply about making a sincere effort to listen without grasping, to respond without reacting, to be willing to learn from each person and each situation.

DON'T BE AN EXPERT

KEY PRACTICES

- Adopt "beginner's mind," or seeing without assuming, anticipating, or judging.
- Embrace failure. Practice "I failed" when things don't go as planned or expected.

- Practice seeing things as if for the first time, such as your hand or while walking.
- Notice mind wandering and rumination.
- Bring awareness to your experiencing self and to your remembering or storytelling self.
- Notice your filters. What stories get in the way of listening?
- Avoid assuming you know what others feel and think; instead, listen to learn what is "invisible" to you.

PRACTICE 4

CONNECT TO YOUR PAIN

There is no coming to consciousness without pain.

— Carl Jung

When I was CEO of the Search Inside Yourself Leadership Institute, I was once invited to attend a dinner in Madison, Wisconsin, a gathering of scientists, leaders, and teachers on the evening before the Dalai Lama was to speak. I was fortunate to be assigned a seat next to Bill George, author of *Discover Your True North* and a professor at the Harvard Business School. During our dinner conversation, he told me something surprising about his experiences working closely with many Fortune 500 CEOs and high-level executives. He noticed that leaders needed to get in touch with their own deep sense of pain, vulnerability, and humility, and occasionally a deep sense of shame, in order to shift from being good leaders to becoming great leaders. At times, this was simply acknowledging the pain of being human, or the pain of feeling like they had let others down, which they had covered up, as many of us do. Other times it was the pain from difficult, imperfect childhoods, failed relationships, or traumatic events.

Feeling this pain helped these executives glimpse how much more was possible by freeing up energy and feelings that were being held close, which allowed them to be more authentic and caring leaders.

This is what mindfulness practice supports and the opportunity it provides. Mindfulness means noticing, staring, looking, and listening to understand what is. This means neither grasping at what we want nor pushing away what we don't like. Neither is necessarily easy to avoid, but the practice of seeing and feeling pain directly, owning it, embodying it, and transforming it can be a particular challenge. However, as Bill George made clear, this practice is often the path from good to great, for it reveals how expansive our hearts can be, which is generally much more than we think. Letting in our pain connects us with our common humanity and with all of life, it strengthens us, and it improves our ability to listen and to act.

When we let ourselves feel the depths of our suffering, paradoxically, we may discover that this space is rather full — full of a deep connection with ourselves and with others; full of hope and meaning, beyond our usual thinking minds.

In truth, *pain* isn't always quite the right word when it comes to this practice. *Empty* at times may be better. Connect to the emptiness, sadness, and lack of control that defines the human condition. This universal pain may be experienced as the pain of our essential aloneness, the pain of change, or the pain that comes from avoiding or resisting change. The pain of not getting what we want or of getting what we don't want. The pain of not being able to control our lives; the pain of aging and of sickness. The pain of wanting to protect our children, families, and friends and knowing that we can't shield anyone from sadness, change, and loss, even ourselves. The pain of unfairness, poverty, cruelty, and violence, both what we witness and what we read or hear about in the world. Finally, it is the pain of knowing that we will lose everything and everyone; people we know will die. We will die.

This is what I mean by the practice "Connect to your pain."

The surprise, however, and what Bill George has seen in the leaders he's worked with, is that what might appear as painful and uncomfortable often holds what is most important in our lives. When we face, feel, and connect with discomfort, we often experience what we most need to learn, what is most meaningful. Turning toward and connecting to my own pain has been essential in helping me discover what is most important, whether in leadership roles or in any part of my life. This is the benefit of the fourth practice, and I've found it true for me again and again.

THE FOUR NOBLE TRUTHS

Connecting to your pain is the first and perhaps most important teaching of the historical Buddha more than 2,500 years ago. It is the first truth of what are called the Four Noble Truths. The first truth states the unavoidable, obvious facts of the world: Discomfort, sickness, old age, and death visit every being, if we are lucky. Time, change, and impermanence are the only things that endure. Everything else ends. It was no news flash even then, but the Buddha's first truth is that being human is truly a tough gig.

The next two truths are a little more unexpected. The second truth says that our discomfort or suffering is not caused by impermanence and emptiness or any situation in itself. Suffering arises from our attempts to avoid discomfort. Then, the third noble truth says that only by owning, connecting with, and transforming discomfort can we be free of it. Skillfully connecting with and navigating change, our pain, and the causes of our pain is the source of our freedom, satisfaction, and happiness.

Finally, the fourth noble truth describes the Buddha's recommended path for doing this. These are practices for seeing all parts of our lives more clearly — our outlook, thinking, mindfulness, speech, action, livelihood, effort, and meditation practice.

Thus, this book's fourth practice, "Connect to your pain," essentially incorporates the Buddha's first three noble truths: Acknowledge and accept what hurts and use that as a guide to identify what's most important and the best actions to take.

I think this is one of the things that made working in a Zen monastery kitchen so powerful and why I still draw lessons about leadership from that time. People who choose to practice Zen are generally not hiding the fact that there is something missing, often something profoundly painful, in their lives. As we worked together in the kitchen, I found this sense of pain was often palpable. And yet, acknowledging this pain, mostly through kindness and connection, right in the midst of the demands of kitchen tasks, was healing, and it led both to the development of character and to producing extraordinary results.

THE BENEFIT OF PAIN: IT ALERTS US TO TROUBLE

This practice of acknowledging and connecting with your emotional discomfort may seem rather strange and counterintuitive. Who wants to be uncomfortable? I don't. I'm not a big fan of physical or emotional pain. I faint easily, not only at the sight of blood, but at the thought of having blood taken. Several years ago I went to see a new doctor, and she asked me, as part of an intake questionnaire, how I respond to shots and needles. Before I could answer, I started to feel mildly lightheaded.

As descendants of the nervous apes, we can be easily overwhelmed by all the existential threats we face. Our feelings and emotional lives are fragile, constantly changing, and outside of our control. No matter how lucky and long our lives may be, the world still steadily chips away at us: family and friends pass, our eyesight deteriorates, our memories go, we can't run like we used to, companies fold and we lose our jobs, others disappoint us, there are too many bills, things break, and so on.

Who wants to face that? But it gets worse. We have inside an inner critic and a worrywart. We suffer when we don't get what we desire, or when we instead get exactly what we don't want. If we don't reach our goals, we beat ourselves up inside; we experience depression, guilt, blame, and other mental and emotional challenges. We experience stress from the constant drama of everyday life.

Our culture and society rarely help us. Much of our current entertainment industry and health care industry appears devoted to avoiding discomfort or immediately addressing the symptoms without fixing the cause. We distract ourselves and medicate ourselves at the first sign of emotional or physical discomfort. In the introduction, I describe the numbness and turning away that defined not only my reaction to discomfort when I was growing up but the reaction of everyone I knew. Some shut down all emotion to avoid feeling pain.

This is a mistake. Being numb and asleep is only the illusion of not feeling pain. We still feel it, and we need to feel it for a very good reason: Pain is helpful.

The truth is, pain serves a useful purpose. Rather than despair when pain inevitably arrives, we might explore welcoming it. Pain helps us identify problems; pain makes sure we don't overlook what has harmed us. We intuitively understand this when it comes to physical pain, but not when it comes to emotional pain and existential crises.

Our bodies are amazingly fragile. We are subject to disease and easily injured. A common cold, toothache, or mild back spasm can make us feel miserable for days. According to the World Health Organization, approximately thirty thousand diseases have been identified by modern medicine, and there are no known cures for three-quarters of them.

And yet, at the first sign of a cold, illness, or injury, we typically seek advice and treatment. If the pain is particularly bad or the symptoms undeniably serious — say, we trip and find our ankle no longer supports our weight — we stop everything. Normal life can't continue until we correctly identify the cause and treat it appropriately. If we don't, if we let that pain go untreated for weeks or months or years, hobbling around and assuring everyone that we're fine, really, no big deal — we know the problem will only get worse till it's beyond healing; till, perhaps, we become crippled for life.

Why don't we treat emotional suffering the same way?

NOT TURNING AWAY: MEDITATE ON YOUR PAIN

When the Buddha says that our freedom and happiness depend on embracing our discomfort, what does that mean? In the West, this discovery was expressed by the Roman emperor

Marcus Aurelius, who famously said, "If you are distressed by anything external, the pain is not due to the thing itself, but to your estimate of it: and this you have the power to revoke at any moment." This sounds good, but how do we transform our discomfort? Not by avoiding it, but by becoming more and more familiar with it.

The most effective way to transform difficulty and pain is by shedding light on the feelings and associations of this pain, to shed light and increase understanding. The same can be said for most emotional and physical pain — greater understanding leads to more choice and more freedom.

I recently met with an executive in a large service company whom I've had a coaching relationship with for many years. He shared with me that his father had recently died. He told me that he was glad to be busy at work so that he didn't have to feel the pain and the loss. I suggested that he explore another strategy — to give himself time to feel his feelings, to process what he appreciated about and what he missed from his father. And to get whatever support he needed from family, friends, or a therapist in order to grieve.

When it comes to emotional pain, the most effective and appropriate response is simply to welcome any pain with acceptance, while noticing any resistance to staying with what is uncomfortable.

Meditation: Observing Pain

Here is a short guided meditation on leaning into what is painful.

Start by finding a way to sit where you can be both relaxed and alert. Gently bring attention to your body, making conscious choices about how to sit. Place your feet flat on the floor. Decide how to place your hands, either palms down or palms up, on your thighs or in your lap. Sit up slightly straighter than normal, putting some energy in the back and spine, slightly arching your back. Relax your shoulders and your jaw. Notice any place where there is holding, and see if you can relax, with some energy.

Now bring your attention to your breath. Just notice without trying to change anything. Notice each inhale and each exhale. Pay particular attention to each exhale.

Now, check in with your thinking mind. Just notice your thoughts, then see if you can bring your attention back to your body or breath.

Now bring your attention to your feelings, whatever you might be feeling right now. Without forcing anything or trying to change anything, allow any feelings of sadness, or longing, or emptiness to arise. Where in your body do you feel emotional discomfort?

After a short time, bring your attention back to your breath and body. How does attention to discomfort influence your breathing? Then return your attention to whatever is next in your day and how you might integrate these practices with your relationships and your work.

NOTICE WHEN YOU'RE OUT OF ALIGNMENT

One form of discomfort or pain arises when our lives are out of alignment with our goals, such as when what we do doesn't fit our values, or when we have changed but our lives have not. When we discover we are out of alignment, we can notice how we describe the events of our lives and the stories we weave to make sense of the world. This is what the imaginative ape is good at.

Becoming aligned with our deepest values, our deepest sense of ourselves, often begins when we notice we are out of alignment. If you notice a sense of disconnection and discomfort in your work, your job, or your career, pay attention to it! Being out of alignment can happen in small ways — noticing that a particular activity or decision is troubling, unsatisfying, or doesn't fit. Or it can happen in more profound ways — realizing that a career or an important relationship has become a regular source of discomfort rather than of satisfaction or joy.

I distinctly remember the day, about fifteen years ago, when I walked into my office at Brush Dance and realized it was time to move on. I had founded the publishing company about fourteen years previously; the company was like a child that I had given birth to and nurtured. It had been a long road, with many ups and downs, especially during the early years when it was a start-up business run from my garage, and yet I was extremely proud of how successfully I had led the company's growth. By this time, we had about fifteen employees, were doing $2.5 million in revenue, and were designing, producing, and distributing greeting cards, calendars, and journals to Borders, Barnes & Noble, Amazon, and Target, as well as to hundreds of retail bookstores and gift shops throughout the world.

Then, one morning at about 8 AM, I arrived at my office, walked to my desk, and was about to sit down when I heard a subtle yet clear, distinct voice that said, *My heart isn't here. This is no longer the place I should be.*

I did not want to hear this voice, and I immediately felt uncomfortable, upset, and pained. If I listened to this voice, it would mean changing everything and giving up not only my creation and my livelihood but a major portion of my identity: as a founder and CEO, as a creator of inspirational products, as a leader in environmental practices, as a successful entrepreneur. I attempted to ignore this voice and hoped that it would go away. After all, who would I be and what would I do if I were not in this role? This was a terrifying thought.

Shortly afterward, I had a memorable breakfast meeting with one of my board members, who was also an investor, friend, and mentor. About fifteen years older than me, Shina Richardson had striking white hair and penetrating blue eyes. She had been the CEO of a successful real estate and pension management company, and she was very intuitive, exuding an aura of depth and mystery.

During breakfast, Shina looked directly into my eyes and said, "Marc, it's time for you to leave Brush Dance."

I assumed she was being critical of me, of my leadership abilities, and I felt ashamed. Before I could collect my thoughts and respond, she continued, "You have much bigger things to do with your life than run this small publishing company."

I immediately felt a sense of relief. I felt lifted up, and at the same time, I felt as though I were being held above the edge of a cliff. I was puzzled and surprised by this comment.

"Like what?" I asked. "What do you mean, I have bigger things to do with my life?"

She said, "That, you will have to figure out. Let's go to a bookstore."

End of conversation.

This meeting, which encouraged me to face the feelings of discomfort I was already experiencing, was the beginning of my search to find a new alignment and a new path in my life. After talking with Shina, I realized a significant chapter was ending and a new one needed to begin. Seeking alignment then led to everything I have done since, and reflecting back, I can't imagine how unhappy I would be if I'd never left Brush Dance. I am grateful for the pain, for the voice that expressed my lack of alignment, for my friend who helped me face my discomfort, and for the courage to stay with the pain and to explore, learn, and grow.

EXPLORE YOUR STORY: CREATE A TIMELINE

I have used this exercise within Google and Search Inside Yourself trainings to help people explore their stories. By identifying and connecting with the highest (or happiest) and the lowest (or most painful) points in your life, you may gain some insight regarding the relationship between these points, and this may help move you toward greater alignment with what is most important for you.

Using a piece of paper and a pen or pencil, draw a straight line across the bottom of the page. On the bottom left, put the year of your birth. On the bottom right, put the current year. Mark the line in ten-year increments. On the top of the page, write, "Times when I felt most happy and successful"; on the bottom, just above the line, write, "Times when I felt least happy and successful." Next, fill in the timeline with whatever incidents, events, and stories come to mind — put the greatest joys and successes on top, noting the years they occurred, and put the greatest difficulties, failures, and losses along the bottom. Overall, I recommend at least ten items and no more than twenty, but it's up to you.

As an example, here is a timeline I created for my own life up to writing this book. Use this for inspiration as you fill out yours.

ON THE TOP

1962 — winning the local Colonia, NJ, Little League World Series, as a pitcher
1976 — enter Tassajara, Zen Mountain Center
1981 — get married
1983 — son, Jason, is born
1986 — complete NYU MBA program
1987 — daughter, Carol, is born
1989 — launch Brush Dance
2004 — launch ZBA Associates and publish first book, *Zen of Business Administration*
2012 — launch SIYLI (Search Inside Yourself Leadership Institute)
2015 — teach mindfulness and emotional intelligence in Japan, with a translator

ON THE BOTTOM

1978 — father dies
1995 — mother dies
2004 — leave Brush Dance
2017 — leave SIYLI

Looking at your timeline of high points and low points, what do you notice? How do you feel remembering the times you felt best and the times you felt worst? Are you surprised by any of your choices or by your responses?

What insights arise? Do you notice either that (1) some of the negative events still sting, still take up both psychic and emotional space, or that (2) some events labeled as negative were actually important transitions that led to positive change?

In my own list, I was very surprised that I had so many

more positive than negative events. My tendency is to think more about the negative. I'm also surprised at the power and intensity that the negative events still have compared to the positive.

Our story is a narrative. As Daniel Kahneman says, we seem to have an experiencing self and a narrative self. This exercise is a way of exploring and learning from how these two parts of you interact.

TRY THIS: Choose one of the moments you identified as a low point on your timeline. Write about this event for at least twelve minutes. Just write, without editing or overthinking. Afterward, read what you wrote. What do you learn? How might these insights positively influence your life?

FEELING MISERABLE ON PURPOSE

When it comes to emotional pain, the strategy I adopted from a very early age was denial and compartmentalization. I grew up with a manic-depressive father, and the tension and anxiety in my house was palpable, yet difficult issues and feelings (any feelings, positive or negative) were rarely addressed. This strategy appeared to be working for my parents, and I felt safe ignoring any emotional tensions in myself and turning my attention outward: to my daily life, to getting good grades, to reading *The Hardy Boys* and other mystery novels, and so on.

Today, I've been practicing Zen meditation for more than forty years. I teach mindfulness and emotional intelligence to leaders and businesspeople around the world. I often divulge to those I am teaching how strange I feel at times, how I struggle in my own life as a leader, husband, and father to embody emotional intelligence. I sometimes divulge that my wife thinks it is rather odd that *I* am teaching emotional intelligence.

To counteract my tendency to compartmentalize and to avoid stress and pain, I've taken on a practice I call feeling miserable on purpose. About once a month during my morning meditation, I deliberately and consciously allow myself to open to all my stress, pain, and discomfort. I think about and feel all of the sadness and emptiness in my own life, in the lives of people around me, and in the world. I just let it all in, as fully and deeply as I can. Strong emotions and tears arise and I embrace them. They come and they go. Often these strong feelings of pain are followed by strong feelings of appreciation and connection.

TRY THIS: Another practice I've recently learned is called "one less breath." Bring awareness that with every breath you take, it is one less breath you have during this lifetime. The purpose of this practice is to appreciate your life right now, to not take anything for granted.

MAINTAIN PERSPECTIVE

I discovered at the end of 2016 that I had prostate cancer, which has since been treated. However, after my initial diagnosis, I did research about this cancer, and I learned that it is very common among men over sixty. Further, the medical community has tended to be overly reactive to it. Now, a large majority of men with prostate cancer fall within a category known as "watchful waiting," meaning that instead of immediately taking action by having surgery or radiation therapy, these men continue to have regular tests and wait to see how (or even whether) the cancer progresses. Prostate cancer can be very slow growing, and some men never need treatment at all.

When I was first tested and diagnosed, I hoped to be in this category. I'm really good at watchful waiting and other forms of avoidance. Unfortunately, my doctor told me — as did two other doctors I met with for a second (and third) opinion — that I did not fall in this category. My cancer was more pronounced and more aggressive. I needed to take action.

While exploring options for treating my prostate cancer, I learned that one common side effect of treatments like surgery and chemotherapy is diminished sexual functioning. This felt rather core to my identity, and it played a significant role as I considered options. Then one of my doctor friends wisely pointed out, "You don't have a very good sex life when you are dead."

Connecting to pain, and a touch of humor, can help a good deal when making challenging decisions, since it helps us maintain perspective.

CONNECT TO YOUR PAIN

KEY PRACTICES

- Face and connect with pain and discomfort, since this helps us learn what is most important and meaningful to us.
- Remember that emotional pain, like physical pain, is a helpful signal about a problem that needs attention.

- Practice meditation as a way of exploring discomfort.
- Notice when your life gets out of alignment; listen to your intuition and feelings of dissatisfaction or discomfort.
- Explore your story and your understanding of positive and negative events by creating a timeline.
- To avoid denial and compartmentalization, occasionally feel miserable on purpose and connect to our shared human condition.
- Practice "one less breath" to appreciate being alive and not taking anything for granted.
- Maintain perspective by not turning away from painful situations.

PART TWO

CONNECT

PRACTICE 5

CONNECT TO THE PAIN OF OTHERS

If you want others to be happy, practice compassion.
If you want to be happy, practice compassion.
— The Dalai Lama

I have been a member of the Social Venture Network (SVN), a nonprofit organization that was an early pioneer in the field of socially responsible business, for more than twenty years, ever since I was CEO of Brush Dance. SVN has more than five hundred members, and it hosts two annual conferences, one on the West Coast each fall and one on the East Coast each spring.

I distinctly remember one of the first SVN conferences I attended just outside of New York City. Several hundred business leaders and CEOs of for-profit and not-for-profit companies were seated in large concentric circles. Ram Dass, an early SVN member, was standing in the middle of the circles, speaking to the group, and facilitating a discussion among the community. When Ram Dass paused, a CEO of a large, successful manufacturing company raised his hand and was handed the microphone. He expressed that he felt like an outsider, even something of an impostor, and that he did not feel as though he belonged in this group. He did not feel as successful nor had his business had enough social impact compared to others for him to be sitting in the circle. Then another longtime member of the group was handed the microphone and expressed that she felt the same way and for similar reasons. As the microphone was passed around, several other prominent members of the group each expressed sharing this feeling of not belonging.

Being new to this community, I was surprised. From my perspective, everyone who spoke was both a successful businessperson and a prominent long-term SVN member. If these people felt like outsiders, then perhaps I and my company — Brush Dance was then a modest fledgling business with revenues under a million dollars — also didn't belong.

When Ram Dass was handed the microphone back, he thanked everyone for their openness and vulnerability. Certainly, he had not asked for nor expected people to voice these doubts, but he listened to them and acknowledged the pain and longing that was so beautifully expressed. Then he suggested we use our pain and vulnerability as the starting point for developing trust and for finding real solutions to the pressing issues of our communities and the wider world.

On some level, I think everyone in the room could relate to the pain of not belonging. I believe it's a universal human desire to want to belong to a group, a cause, a community, to something larger than our individual self. This is what the empathic ape seeks — connection — and we experience pain when we are excluded or when we feel like we don't quite fit, like we don't quite belong. We suffer when we feel disconnected, whether one on one or as part of a group, and this sense of loss might also be universal. At some point, everyone feels alone, separate, an outsider.

At this SVN conference, the group's shared expression of pain, isolation, and longing, this feeling that something was lacking, actually brought everyone together. We felt connected by our common human desire for connection. The remainder of the day and for the following days of the conference, the community felt close and intimate — we shared the intimacy of fellow misfits, of those who become connected if only through the feeling of not belonging. This was an unexpected and paradoxical result: Everyone felt more connected through the group's shared vulnerability and need to belong.

TRY THIS: Write about your own feelings of belonging and not belonging.

What groups do you belong to?
When do you feel as though you don't belong?
What undercuts your feelings of belonging?
What supports your feelings of belonging?

LEADERSHIP MEANS FOSTERING COMMUNITY AND CONNECTION

The fifth practice in this book may be one of the most important competencies in the art of stellar leadership as well as in creating a more peaceful world. I've experienced often the transformation that can occur in a short amount of time when people deeply see one another and open to our shared humanity: to the universal desire to be happy and connected and to the universal experience of pain when we are not. The potent practice "Connect to the pain of others" is key for leaders as they cultivate a group's sense of purpose and as they foster the personal development and inner strength of each member.

Like practice 4, the "pain" referred to in this practice is really the universal human experience of discomfort and loss. While it includes physical pain and each person's individual circumstances, the deeper focus is recognizing the type of emotional pain everyone shares: of impermanence, of change, of disconnection, and of the awareness of impending loss, old age, sickness, and death. And it includes the pain that is particular to our sense of self — feeling like a separate individual and yet aspiring to be connected within a community.

As descendants of the empathic ape, we evolved and are built to feel the emotions of others. This is the definition of empathy, and it includes all feeling states, both physical and emotional. Indeed, we are connected to others beyond what we usually realize or imagine, which a host of scientific research has shown. We are influenced by the hormones and body chemistry of others, to the extent that women who live together tend to have synchronized menstrual cycles. It's proven that positive and negative emotions can be contagious. These things reflect our common, shared experience so much that it almost goes without saying that our feelings and emotions are powerfully interconnected.

A mistake we can make is thinking we don't have to share the pain of others. This is particularly true for leaders, and there is some evidence that greater leadership authority is correlated with a decrease in empathy. Somehow, though humans are built to recognize emotion in one another, we sometimes think we can remain separate from it. Why do we do this? I'm not sure, but there are several likely reasons. One is that separation can seem to free us from obligation: If you are separate from me, and your pain is not my pain, then I don't have to do anything about it. Another common reason is probably that we don't want to feel *our own* pain. We may go to great lengths not to experience or share someone else's pain, such as their loneliness or grief, since that means admitting to our own. This is why being an empathic ape is easier when others are happy and much harder when they are not.

Yet empathy is a core competency of leadership, a vital part of being human, and part of our common humanity. As I hope you'll find, learning to skillfully connect with the pain of others actually, and paradoxically, supports and increases our ability to feel a deep sense of safety and satisfaction; it fosters a profound feeling of belonging. It ultimately enables our freedom to express our deepest truths and help others express theirs. This practice is aimed at training your mind and heart to connect more deeply with others by acknowledging and experiencing other people's experience and perspectives, to see and feel our human similarities, and to cultivate compassion, or the practice of offering kindness.

RECOGNIZE THE FOUR HORSEMEN

Dr. John Gottman studies the factors that lead married couples either to remain together or to divorce, and he has demonstrated that after observing couples for five minutes, he has a greater than 90 percent chance of predicting which couples will stay together and which will split apart. Dr. Gottman names four behaviors as key indicators for predicting which marriages will not survive: criticism, contempt, defensiveness, and stonewalling. He calls these the Four Horsemen of the Apocalypse.

These are very familiar behaviors that can show up at any time in any relationship. These four behaviors name ways that we actively avoid connecting to another person's pain. They are effective strategies and behaviors for shutting us off from others. In order to develop your capacity for connecting to the pain of others, it's useful to learn to recognize these horsemen, so that you uncover your methods of avoidance.

Even though nearly everyone engages in these negative behaviors at some time, I think it's worth defining them to clarify the strategies they employ.

CRITICISM — Making disapproving judgments. Often this is a way to show that the other person's pain is their fault, which relieves us of an obligation to help.

CONTEMPT — To despise or dishonor; to question someone's honesty or integrity. This is usually used to deny the pain or undermine its validity. We don't have to share what doesn't exist.

DEFENSIVENESS — Putting up barriers to avoid a challenge or criticism; disagreeing over circumstances or facts. Like criticism, this is usually used to deny fault or personal responsibility and thus our obligation to help.

STONEWALLING — Delaying or blocking by refusing to answer questions or by giving evasive replies. In other words, when all else fails, we simply ignore what we don't want to see or deal with.

TRY THIS: How do you usually avoid someone else's pain? Take a moment to consider the "Four Horsemen" — criticism, contempt, defensiveness, and stonewalling — and see if one or two name your preferred strategy. Mine is stonewalling. When I'm feeling vulnerable and connecting with my own pain, my first tendency is to close down. I want to run away or disappear, so I retreat, stonewalling, until I feel safe enough to engage. For the rest of the week, or whenever you think of it, be on the lookout for these horsemen, both in yourself and others. Sometimes their appearance is subtle, sometimes obvious. Then, when you notice one showing up in your life, experiment with doing the opposite: Feel someone else's pain and focus on connection, not exclusion or difference.

A MORE PEACEFUL WORLD: SEEING SIMILARITIES, OFFERING KINDNESS

As the cofounder and former CEO of the Search Inside Yourself Leadership Institute, I helped craft SIYLI's vision and mission statement, which is: "All leaders in the world are wise and compassionate, thus creating the conditions for world peace."

When creating this statement, the SIYLI board felt that it was important to aim high (very high!) and to articulate an audacious vision and mission that might even appear impossible. That seems fitting for the audacious and impossible times we live in and for teaching practices of mindfulness and emotional intelligence. However, I've sometimes seen people roll their eyes and dismiss such an impossibly naive, aspirational statement. Indeed, given the track record of human civilization as well as the existing state of violence, conflict, and wars around our planet, can you blame them? Where are these wise, compassionate leaders? How can any individual ever foster conditions for world peace?

Yet this practice in particular, connecting to the pain of others, is what gives me hope.

For instance, a highlight of the Search Inside Yourself two-day mindfulness and emotional intelligence program takes place at the end of the morning of the second day. In many ways, the first day and a half of the program are preparation for this moment: creating a safe environment, teaching participants to sit with more stillness and focus, and practicing listening without interrupting. By now, three emotional intelligence competencies have been introduced: self-awareness, self-management, and motivation. At this point participants are ready to take a deep dive into the practice of connecting to the pain of others. In particular, we practice two core skills: seeing similarities and offering kindness.

Here is the exercise we use, which has been modified for this book. The exercise has two parts: Part 1 focuses on seeing similarities, and part 2 on offering kindness. In workshops, people are paired up and do this exercise while sitting and facing each other. If you decide to do that, I recommend asking someone you trust and are close to, and to have them read this chapter so they understand the context and goals of the exercise. However, this exercise can also be done virtually with another person (such as over the phone or via video conference), and it can be practiced alone: Simply imagine sitting across from whoever you choose, whether a real or imaginary person, and imagine them speaking the script below.

Part 1: Seeing Similarities

Begin with a few minutes of settling, or mindfulness meditation. Bring attention to your body and breath, and let go of the busyness and activities of the day.

Then become aware of the person sitting in front of you. Take a moment to look at this person. They are a human being...just like you. Notice your connection as human beings, and notice whether you feel comfortable with this thought or whether it raises some discomfort. Feel free to maintain eye contact or not.

Then read each of the following sentences, either speaking them out loud or saying them silently in your head. Take your time and consider each statement as it's spoken.

- This person in front of me has a body and a mind... just like me.
- This person in front of me has feelings and thoughts... just like me.
- This person in front of me has experienced pain, sadness, has been angry, hurt, and confused... just like me.
- This person in front of me has experienced physical and emotional pain and suffering... just like me.
- This person in front of me wishes to be free from pain and suffering... just like me.
- This person in front of me has experienced many joys and times of happiness... just like me.
- This person in front of me wishes to be healthy, loved, and have fulfilling relationships... just like me.
- This person in front of me wishes to be happy... just like me.

Part 2: Offering Kindness

Now practice offering kindness. Allow good wishes to arise. Before you begin, take a moment to look at this person again. They are a human being... just like you.

Then, either speaking out loud or silently in your head, read the following statements, taking a pause between each one.

- I wish for this person in front of me to have the strength and the resources to navigate the difficulties in life.
- I wish for this person in front of me to be free from pain and suffering.
- I wish for this person in front of me to be happy.
- Because this person is a fellow human being...just like me.

Next, extend your wishes to others, to all others you can think of, being as bold in your generosity as you can be. If you want, name specific people in these statements, or name other communities you want to include.

- May everyone in this room, building, or house be happy; may they be free from suffering, may they be at peace.
- May my family and friends be happy; may they be free from suffering, may they be at peace.
- May my coworkers and colleagues and all the people I work with be happy; may they be free from suffering, may they be at peace.
- May all beings in the world be happy; may they be free from suffering, may they be at peace.
- Finally, I remember to include myself. May I be happy; may I be free from suffering, may I be at peace.

When you finish speaking, bring your attention to your body and breath. Let go of any thoughts and feelings. Notice that you are breathing in and breathing out. When you both are done and ready, allow a few minutes to bring your attention back to the room.

This exercise can build understanding and create bridges, even between those who are meeting for the first time or who misunderstand or may be in conflict with each other. I believe that one way to create a more peaceful world would be to create a safe space and then do this exercise with the people who feel disconnected and separate from one another.

These two practices, seeing similarities and offering kindness, are incredibly rich in terms of building inner resources and incredibly valuable for loosening our fears and biases and allowing us to see that we are all one tribe, one family — the human family.

LOOKING UNDER THE HOOD

Often our conversations go like this: How are you? Fine. How are you feeling? Fine. How is work, school, your relationships? Fine. A psychologist friend has suggested that FINE could be an acronym standing for "feelings inside not expressed."

In other words, *fine* is a socially acceptable form of stonewalling or being defensive. We don't have to accept *fine* as an answer, though. We can recognize this gentle form of avoidance and do what I sometimes call *looking under the hood*: Rather than just skim the surface of feelings, we can encourage people to be real and share their transitions, challenges, and pain. We can be curious about and face, rather than avoid, fears and doubts, including our own. Without prying, and with respect, we might explore the myriad difficulties and challenges of life, including the feeling that we don't belong and that we often feel safer hiding what hurts. It can be surprising and powerful to uncover the pains and concerns of others, which live just under the surface of daily life. This pain is the glue that connects us, the emotional resonance of what every human being shares — our struggles, failures, vulnerability, and suffering; our common humanity.

For instance, with Norman Fischer, I have been co-leading Company Time one-day workshops for businesspeople at Green Gulch Farm for more than twenty years. We usually meet three or four times per year, and each time, about half the people have attended previous Company Time workshops and half are attending for the first time. Early in the morning, everyone introduces themselves, and people's titles and work biographies are often very impressive: They are CEOs, scientists, entrepreneurs, coaches, consultants, and other high-profile professionals. Then, after we practice meditation and mindful listening and everyone begins to feel more safe and vulnerable, we check in again later in the day. This time, nearly everyone volunteers their struggles; nearly everyone is in some kind of transition at work or in their personal life. In the morning, there is a sense that people want to appear impressive, which results in comparisons and a lack of connection. In the afternoon, people become much more vulnerable and open about their struggles and pains, which results in connection, trust, and empathy. I've found this same pattern is equally true in business and nonbusiness environments.

As another example, several years ago I led a one-day mindfulness and emotional intelligence training for a group of one hundred top salespeople for a major software company just outside of Austin, Texas. It was a two-day meeting: Day one was meant to provide strategies for working in a stressful environment and to increase trust and collaboration among this group, and the second day would focus on company strategy and goals.

As I stood onstage and looked around at the participants, everyone appeared successful and self-assured. The group was quite diverse, with men and women from many different countries in Asia and North and South America. The men were mostly wearing suits and ties, and women were dressed in semiformal business attire. The room exuded an air of confidence and success.

By the middle of the morning — after exploring several of the mindfulness and listening exercises from the first four practices of this book — everyone began to let go of their game faces. People dropped their roles and expertise and revealed their vulnerabilities as people.

They asked more questions, and their questions became more personal. Many asked how to work with stress in the midst of high demands and about the challenges of working virtually with teams around the world, while others asked about managing lots of travel with family life, how to handle anxiety attacks, and how to be emotionally present with their families after a stress-filled workday. A few asked for help with behavior and drug-related issues that their children were confronting. One woman shared with me that she had been grieving since her youngest daughter died in a car accident.

By the end of the day, the energy in the room had changed palpably. The group felt open, connected, and trusting. They were becoming wise, compassionate leaders creating the conditions of peace.

As Plato said, "Be kind, for everyone you meet is fighting a hard battle."

TRY THIS: Look for opportunities to look under the hood of other people. When meeting someone at a party or business gathering, instead of talking about the weather or other small talk, try asking: *Please tell me your story*. Politely but sincerely ask: *What are some of your biggest challenges? How did you get to be doing what you are doing? What obstacles did you overcome?*

Then just listen, while seeing similarities and offering kindness.

TONGLEN: GIVING AND RECEIVING

Tonglen is an ancient Buddhist practice that is translated as "giving and receiving." Like the exercise above, this practice has two parts. The first part is relatively easy: We send our wishes of peace, freedom, and healing to our family and loved ones, our closest friends, and those we work with. To stretch this muscle of generosity, this practice generally also includes sending these wishes to those we find challenging, people we are in conflict with, and even our most difficult relationships or enemies. Wishing others well is a powerful way of calming the nervous ape.

The second part of tonglen practice can be more challenging. This is the practice of bringing to mind pain and difficulty and touching it, breathing it in, and holding it in our heart. We feel both the pain we are aware of as well as the pain that we can only sense or imagine. This can include times we or others were hurt, let down, or disappointed — from small disappointments, such as not being accepted to a sports team or being treated badly by a friend — to the death of a relative or someone else close.

Thus, this two-part practice begins with the imaginative ape and then engages the empathic ape. It is a way to connect to and transform our relationship with the pain of others, and it is a way to help open our hearts. Doing it provides the experience, both physically and mentally, that our heart, our ability to feel other people's pain, is much larger and more receptive than we generally realize or admit. This practice allows us to be more open and attuned to the challenges and pain of others.

Giving and Receiving Meditation

First, find a way to sit where you can be both relaxed and alert. Take a few minutes to settle your body and mind; check in with your body, your breath, your thoughts and feelings. Then bring your attention to your breath.

Begin by sending good wishes to others. Bring to mind those closest to you, your family, partner, closest friends. Say to yourself: *May they be happy, may they be free from suffering, may they be at peace.*

Now bring to mind your acquaintances and people you work with, and send them good wishes in the same way.

Next, bring to mind people you come into contact with but have little or no relationship with, and do the same.

Finally, bring to mind someone you are in conflict with, and send them good wishes.

When you are finished, shift to the second part of the meditation: Allow yourself to feel the pain of others and the pain of the world. Imagine doing this in whatever way that works for you, whether by bringing specific situations to mind or just allowing all of the losses, grief, inequalities, and difficulties of people you know (and don't know) to arise.

As you do, breathe gently. With each inhale, breathe in the pain and suffering of others and the world, and feel your heart opening and widening. Then, as you exhale, let go of your feelings and bring your attention to your breath. Continue for as long as you wish.

When you are finished, allow a few moments to bring your awareness back to your breath and body, letting go of any thoughts, images, and emotions. Then gently bring your attention back to the room.

LEADING WITH COMPASSION

Not just as leaders but as human beings, fostering empathy is important because it inspires one of the most powerful motivations we have: compassion, or acting with the intention to help reduce the pain of others. Empathy is a potent way to develop inner strength. If we don't see the pain of others, or we refuse to acknowledge it, we won't act to help them. This squanders our power, or our ability to transform the world. With compassion, we can do the opposite. We can use our power for good works, but that first requires this book's fifth practice, connecting to the pain of others.

One question I'm regularly asked is to clarify the difference between empathy and compassion. Empathy is feeling another's feelings and distinguishing their feelings from our own. The second portion of the definition, distinguishing their feelings, is important. Without this distinction, the result is emotional contagion. We go beyond feeling and instead identify with another's feelings.

Compassion has three components: (1) empathy, or feeling another's feelings; (2) understanding, or the aspiration to understand another's feelings and experience; and (3) motivation, or the aspiration to relieve the other person's suffering.

During the Search Inside Yourself two-day training program, we sometimes show a video to give participants the experience of compassion. The video features a young woman singing the "Star-Spangled Banner," the U.S. national anthem, before an NBA basketball game. During the early part of the song, the woman forgets the words and freezes in embarrassment. One of the basketball team's coaches, Maurice Cheeks, steps forward and joins her, so she is no longer standing there alone. He seems to barely know the words, and singing is clearly not his forte, but his support helps to jog her memory, allowing her to continue and complete the song, which ends in celebratory cheers throughout the arena.

Each time I watch this video — and I've now seen this clip more than twenty times — I still feel the woman's terror and embarrassment, and I also feel moved by experiencing the compassion of another person boldly stepping in to help her during her vulnerability and distress.

TRY THIS: In a journal, write about the ways you help others, or could or might help others, in all areas of your life. What supports you and what gets in the way of compassionate actions?

PAIN AND ACCEPTANCE

When I was twenty-six years old and a Zen student living at Green Gulch Farm in Northern California, I learned that my father was hospitalized and quite ill with cancer. I immediately flew to New Jersey to see him. When I arrived at the hospital, I discovered that he was literally tied to his bed. A doctor told me that he was walking around the hospital hallways at night, and they therefore needed to both medicate him and restrain him.

Fortunately, I had an excellent support system. Two of my closest friends from the San Francisco Zen Center were helping me to navigate this difficult and complicated time along with the hospital system. They suggested that I was in charge, not the doctors. With their support, I spoke with my father's doctors, I untied my father from his bed, and I instructed the doctors to stop the medication. Once the drugs wore off and my father became more conscious, I was able to have a real heart-to-heart conversation with him. I let him know the doctor's full prognosis: that his body was filled with cancer and that he most likely did not have long to live. At the same time, I told him that I held out hope, the possibility that anything could happen. I was connecting to my father's pain as fully as I could, and I felt him connecting to how painful it was for me to be having this conversation.

My father had been very disappointed and angry with me ever since I had chosen to live at the Zen Center because I had dropped out of college to do so. In that moment, as I was laying out to my father what was happening, he looked at me and said, "I don't understand what you are doing. But whatever it is, keep doing it."

This was one of the most powerful and meaningful meetings in my life — meeting my father, in our mutual pain, and experiencing how connecting to each other's pain created new understanding and a deep feeling of acceptance and love.

CONNECT TO THE PAIN OF OTHERS
KEY PRACTICES

- Remember that a leader's job, by definition, is to cultivate community and connection.
- Recognize the "Four Horsemen" that seek to avoid connecting to the pain of others: criticism, contempt, defensiveness, and stonewalling.
- Practice seeing similarities and offering kindness.
- In conversation, look under the hood of others by asking about difficulties and challenges.
- Practice tonglen, or giving and receiving meditation.
- Foster empathy in order to inspire, and lead with, acts of compassion.

PRACTICE 6

DEPEND ON OTHERS

A hundred times every day I remind myself that my inner and outer life are based on the labors of other men, living and dead, and that I must exert myself in order to give in the same measure as I have received and am still receiving.

— Albert Einstein

One of the most memorable aspects during my time leading a Zen monastery kitchen was our team menu-planning sessions. Each week I would sit down with three guest cooks. These were students chosen from those working in the kitchen who were the most experienced and talented chefs. During the summer they were responsible for preparing three meals each day for the monastery's seventy to eighty overnight guests. On our table were stacks of vegetarian cookbooks, detailed records of previous menus, and lots of ideas written on various sheets of paper and index cards. Our task was to decide every meal and menu, along with who would do what, for every day of the following week. Some meals were chosen from our standard tried-and-true offerings. Others were more experimental; we sometimes wanted to stretch ourselves and try new ideas, along with wanting to use and highlight in-season vegetables and fruits.

As head cook, my primary role during these sessions was

to act as a coach and mentor. I provided feedback about what was working well and what could be better. We addressed the culture and practice of the kitchen and how the team was functioning and growing. In particular, we discussed how each cook was developing and learning, both from a practice perspective and as a cook. Then, we discussed the quality of the meals — what was working well and what could be better about the food that we served. As a coach and guide, I would often inquire about what I could do to support them, both individually and as a team, and what I could do to support the overall practice and effectiveness of the kitchen.

I found these meetings to be satisfying and sometimes even exhilarating. As a team, we experienced a high level of trust and care, which arose from working and practicing together both inside and outside of the kitchen. A core practice of Zen is generosity — being attentive and kind with ourselves and with one another. Thus, our job in a Zen kitchen was to help one another grow and succeed. When conflicts and disagreements arose, and of course they did, generosity provided a framework and a practice for finding creative solutions. This led to open, strategic discussions regarding the challenges and opportunities of cooking and practicing mindfulness in the kitchen. Whatever our roles, we were all peers learning and growing together by supporting one another. As for the food, we almost always came up with simple, elegant, creative menus that none of us could have planned alone.

These menu-planning meetings combined dedicated and integrated practice: They were both preparation for the primary event of cooking meals (which would happen later), and in themselves they were an important event in which we integrated everything we were learning about working together, supporting one another, and building trust. In these meetings, one of the most important things was noticing and improving how we worked together in order to support one another and get things done. Without that, we never could have fed the monastery's guests to the high standards we aspired to.

This is the heart of what practice 6, "Depend on others," is all about. When it comes time to lead and work with a group, we use and build upon all the practices introduced so far and apply them in order to work well together. This requires a high level of self-awareness and self-confidence, as well as humility, empathy, and openness, or approaching situations with beginner's mind. In many ways, I would say that mindful leadership is really the art of depending on others.

INTERDEPENDENCE: THE ART AND SCIENCE OF LEADERSHIP

A classic definition of leadership is inspiring others to perform and achieve a shared vision. This is true, but I would rephrase this definition of leadership as the art of building trust and meaningful connections in an environment where results matter. The leader is in charge of supporting the team, and this requires interdependence: being in relationship with others who depend on you just as you depend on them.

A key role of a leader is to encourage people to develop their individual skills and perspectives as well as to build a team that contains all the skills and perspectives the team needs to fulfill its goals. This means identifying creative gaps within the team itself, including yourself as the leader. Where might your own skills and perspective be lacking? Who or what does the team need that you can't provide? In other words, "depend on others" as a practice means displaying the understanding, initiative, and responsiveness to create a team that will, collectively, achieve more and think more creatively than the leader or any individual ever could working alone. The group depends on the leader to listen, to respect and consider everyone's ideas and insights, and then to make decisions that are in the best interests of the team and the organization.

In fact, at their best, when groups work well, they almost don't seem to have or need a "leader" at all. At one time, this is what Google believed, and in 2008, they decided to conduct a study called Google Oxygen on what makes great managers — but they were basically hoping to prove that managers don't have much influence in the success of teams. Google's culture, especially in the early years, primarily valued engineering savvy and creativity. Leadership and management were thought of as necessary evils or, at best, unnecessary layers of bureaucracy.

Much to their surprise, Google discovered that the behavior of the leader does significantly matter in both the productivity of the team and the well-being of the team members. Google found that leaders from the most successful, highly rated teams all shared three common behaviors:

- **COACHING:** A good leader takes the time to meet with each person on the team and act as a coach, which involves both building trust with and also challenging each team member. A good leader demonstrates real care for each person and for their career development.
- **EMPOWERMENT:** A good leader empowers the team and avoids micromanaging — guiding and supporting the team, trusting the team to do what's

required, and providing the team with a good deal of freedom. A good leader seeks the balance of providing what the team needs to succeed while being careful to not frustrate or get in the way of the team's functioning by managing too closely.

- **LISTENING:** A good leader creates an inclusive environment and shows concern for both success and well-being by listening to each team member. A good leader brings awareness to any inherent tensions between the team's success, the company's success, and the individual's well-being and finds ways to resolve them and support success on all levels.

What Google discovered in their study is very similar to how I define (in chapter 1) the three jobs of leaders — to think, listen, and hold space. Whatever terms you prefer, it's also clear that these three jobs or behaviors reflect how mindful leaders compensate for and overcome the sometimes negative impact of the three apes: Leaders pay attention to avoid reactivity and micromanaging, they listen to others to strategize in the best ways for the group, and they foster connection and empathy to avoid a protective tendency to go it alone.

RESISTANCE: TRYING TO SWIM ALONE IN A SEA OF RELATIONSHIPS

When we look at ourselves in the mirror, we appear to be separate, alone, and disconnected. This is a mirage, much like aspen trees that, above ground, appear to be individual trees. Underneath the ground, aspen trees are connected by a massive root system. Similarly, when we look at our fingers, of course, each can move separately. At the same time, they are part of a system, one hand. Humans are much more like this than we generally think. There is an expression from Zen that says we are like water and milk; mixed together they become indistinguishable, not exactly two, not exactly one.

The truth is, we swim in a sea of relationships — with partners, children, parents, siblings, bosses, boards, coworkers, employees, teachers, students, customers, and all the other people who make up our world. We are dependent on others for all the physical and material things that surround us — for our houses, electricity, clothing, and food. Even the clean air or not-so-clean air we breathe depends on others. Every aspect of our world — the health of our families, communities, political systems, and our planet — is interdependent.

This interdependence goes beyond what is obvious — beyond companionship, love, food, clothing. We also depend on others for music, math, politics, science, the arts, our ethics, beliefs, and ideas. Most of us cannot prove that the earth revolves around the sun. We didn't create existentialism, or language, or the internet.

On the most fundamental levels, we are dependent on others for who we are, our identities, our values, how we think, and how we experience ourselves and the world. We are shaped and influenced by our families, our friends, our community, our education, our religion (or lack of a religious tradition), and our society. The degree to which we exist in a web of ideas and beliefs and community is difficult to fully appreciate with our conscious minds.

Yet, strangely enough, what we often celebrate the most is independence. To be number one, as if all that counts is a single raised digit and not the whole hand. We feel we should be able to take care of ourselves, to make it on our own, to be self-made men and women who aren't beholden to others for our livelihood, welfare, or circumstances. Of course, personal strength, confidence, and self-reliance are excellent qualities, but those qualities don't exist in isolation. They aren't meant to separate and divide us from others. Just as Google discovered that all teams need good managers to thrive, an individual's successful independence reflects the support of their wider community.

If that's true, then why is it that we so often forget the fact of our interdependence or seek to avoid depending on others? First of all, recognizing our dependence can be risky and frightening. Depending on others includes the potential for disappointment and the pain of being let down and hurt. Any close business, personal, or family relationship means relying or depending on others to show up, to help, to do the jobs you can't do, to provide emotional support, to accept you, to love you.

When we depend on others, we can feel vulnerable. Others might fail us, causing loss and pain. Since no one wants to be hurt, we might try to avoid being dependent or admitting how dependent we really are. If we do this (or more often, *when* we do this), our attitudes are really a defense against being hurt rather than seeking an achievement that reflects on and benefits our community, or all the people who support us.

Further, being in relationship means that we are not in control. Others may have different goals, or different ideas about how to reach those goals, and yet we can't move forward without other people. Agreement, cooperation, and collaboration can be difficult to achieve, and so simply in order to get things done, it can sometimes seem easier to do things alone. If we believe in our expertise, we might also believe that the only or the best way to get things done is our way, and so we avoid discussions, negotiations, and compromises.

Practice 6, "Depend on others," can bring up a lot of resistance. The nervous ape doesn't like being vulnerable, and so the nervous ape often resists dependence in all its forms. The imaginative ape easily comes up with worst-case scenarios, spinning all kinds of stories about what could go wrong or how we might be found lacking. The risks of depending on others are tremendous, almost never-ending, and yet they mostly boil down to a few simple fears: Perhaps that, if we rely on others, they may turn into threats who seek to undermine or harm us (through their actions or inaction). Or that others will eventually, and inevitably, let us down by abandoning us, leaving us for a better job or a better partner, or simply by becoming ill or dying.

Whatever the reasons, the ways we act to protect ourselves in our relationships are fairly easy to recognize. We shield our feelings and our hearts from depending on others by doing exactly what we fear others will do to us.

- We don't fully commit to a relationship or a group.
- We aspire to be strong and independent as a way to show we don't really need a relationship or a group.
- We constantly search for another, better relationship (for better employees, partners, friends) or a better job; that is, we hedge our bets and withhold trust.

These actions lead away from connection by fostering disconnection. They can undermine our strengths, since they are ways we refuse help, and so they diminish any help we might receive. Emotionally, they sacrifice richness for shallowness in the name of self-protection, as a way to avoid disappointment and heartbreak. They represent an approach to independence that actually hampers the results we long for.

In business, leaders face this dilemma all the time as part of their job: They fear being let down by those they lead and looking bad as a result. This is why I think of depending on others as an art that in many ways defines what mindful leadership is all about. Depending on others requires practicing and cultivating all six of the other mindfulness practices.

As a small positive example of this, when I was CEO of the Search Inside Yourself Leadership Institute, I decided to initiate an open vacation policy. This meant that employees could take as much time off as they wanted for retreats or well-being, without any limit. The only agreement was that everyone would complete their work and meet or exceed agreed-upon goals and performance standards. There was no approval process for time off, other than coordinating vacations among employees. This was important to me, both personally and for the company culture. I didn't want anyone tracking my vacation time. I wanted to be supported and trusted, and I wanted to treat others in the same way.

At first, I noticed that I felt nervous and vulnerable about this policy. I wondered if employees would abuse it. I worried that I'd be seen as not creating a sense of urgency and accountability or that I'd be viewed as a pushover. This anxiety remained for several months, and in a few cases, people who were not meeting their work obligations had to be let go. Eventually, this policy, and several others that empowered employees and gave people lots of freedom, helped shape a culture that was dynamic, productive, and caring. Not only did employees not abuse the policy, they tended to not take enough time off. I had to remind people to do retreats and take vacations. And the level of commitment to our work and to the team was extremely high, often off the charts.

One of the more interesting lessons I learned from our open vacation policy was that by providing more openness and trust, I also needed to be more conscious and disciplined about agreed-upon results, as well as to have difficult conversations when results were not being achieved. Depending on others, when done well, can help achieve a paradoxical blend: It allows for more freedom and greater empowerment while encouraging greater clarity, accountability, and results.

TRY THIS: Just notice the ways that you find it difficult to depend on others. What is your edge? In what ways is depending on others challenging? In what ways are you vulnerable to being let down, disappointed, and hurt? Notice your resistance, your reluctance to being open and vulnerable. Where in your body does this reluctance and resistance appear? Journal about your answers.

MEDITATING ALONE TOGETHER

Here is the question I am asked most frequently by Google engineers about mindfulness meditation: "What is the least amount of time I can meditate and have it make a difference?" I respond that the majority of scientific studies measuring the effectiveness of meditation are based on twenty minutes a day for eight weeks. Other studies report that much shorter amounts of meditation can influence brain structure and behavior patterns. From another perspective, that of my own experience, one conscious, mindful breath each day can make a difference.

The second-most-often-asked question by Google engineers is, "How can I sustain a daily mindfulness meditation practice?" My answer: If possible, practice with others — find another person or a group to sit with. Sitting with others even weekly can make a substantial difference in supporting your practice.

In other words, even meditation and mindfulness depend on others. I experienced this when I first participated in early morning meditation at the San Francisco Zen Center when I was twenty-two years old. I was living in the Sunset district of San Francisco, a few miles west of the Zen Center, and I drove across town at 5:00 AM for the 5:25 AM period of meditation. I walked into the meditation hall and sat down on a black cushion facing the wall. To my left was a woman who seemed over twice my age. She was wearing a light brown poncho. There were two thirty-minute periods of meditation and ten minutes of walking meditation in between. At the end of the second period, we all walked upstairs for twenty minutes of chanting. Afterward, I drove back to my apartment in the Sunset district.

The next morning I drove across the quiet, early morning streets of San Francisco, walked into the meditation hall, and sat in the same seat. To my left was the same woman wearing a light brown poncho. The following morning, when my alarm went off, I felt tired and had the thought of sleeping in instead of going to meditation. Then, I thought, *Oh, the woman in the brown poncho might miss me*. With some resistance, I got out of bed and went to sit meditation, and there she was. My assumption that she was depending on me, even in this most insignificant manner (in my imagination), helped me establish my daily sitting practice. For all I know, I helped her as well.

During the first years of my daily meditation practice, I always sat with groups, which generally ranged from forty to eighty people, at the Zen Center in San Francisco, Tassajara, or Green Gulch Farm (the three centers that comprise the San Francisco Zen Center). The underlying philosophy in which I was trained is that the motivation and rationale for having a meditation practice is multilayered. Cultivating one's inner strength and finding freedom from the egoistic self is a core factor. Two other factors are primary as well: We meditate to support one another's practice. Our presence and intention helps others. And we meditate to develop our ability to listen and respond to others with more depth, which increases our capacity to help them.

That is, meditation and mindfulness are not sought for our personal benefit alone, and they aren't achieved solely through individual effort. The same is true of leadership.

TRY THIS: If you find it difficult to sustain a regular or daily meditation practice on your own, find a buddy, another person to sit with each morning, either in person or virtually. Or find a group to sit with, even once a week. Sitting once a week with others can make a big difference in supporting your daily practice.

When others depend on you to show up, you are more likely to meditate. And sitting with others provides a wider experience of meditation and opens up your overall purpose and intention for practice. Of course, we practice for ourselves, and by sitting with others we find that we also practice to support others. We recognize that our intention and presence supports others' intentions and presence.

LEADERSHIP CREATES COMMUNITY AND EMPOWERS OTHERS

People often think that leadership means doing, and doing whatever is needed, all by yourself. Popular culture fosters the image of the singular hero going it alone: from James Bond to Charlize Theron in the movie *Atomic Blonde* to former Apple CEO Steve Jobs. This was certainly the case for me when I started and grew my first two companies, Brush Dance and ZBA Associates. I had a strong desire and tendency to want to do everything myself. Despite my experiences in a Zen kitchen, it was years before I developed the experience and confidence to regularly depend on others and consistently empower a team. The popular notion of the independent leader is hard to shake, and it can become a bad habit, one I'm still unlearning.

For instance, a number of years ago, within a short time span, several friends and colleagues told me they were interested in participating in a weekly meditation group. They were eager to develop a regular meditation practice, and they believed that being part of a weekly group would support this. Of course, I wholeheartedly agreed, and I decided to launch a meditation group in my hometown and call it Mill Valley Zen. It felt natural for me to lead this effort to support others.

So I rented a room at a local community center, and each Wednesday night we met. I led the meditation and followed this with an informal talk and group discussion. Then after a few months, one by one, everyone in the original group stopped coming — for a variety of reasons, such as new jobs, new relationships, general busyness — and other people joined, and a small community evolved.

Despite my full-time work, I took my role as meditation

leader seriously, and each week, I prepared something to say, or sometimes I would read passages from a Zen-related book. I also got into the routine of doing everything involved in the administration of the group: I paid the weekly rent at the community center, unlocked the doors before our meetings, collected the donations, and locked the doors after our meetings. When I was traveling and couldn't attend, I arranged for an experienced teacher to substitute for me to lead the group.

Years went by. While I found the group very nourishing, at other times it felt like a good deal of effort. After seven years the group began to feel somewhat burdensome to me, and one Wednesday evening I announced to the group that I wanted to take a break, a long break, like forever.

A few days later I received an email from one of the group members inviting me to meet for dinner before the following Wednesday group meeting. Eight people attended the dinner, and they informed me that they did not accept my resignation. They wanted to find a way to allow me to teach and not have other responsibilities. They decided to take away my checkbook and pay the rent (from weekly donations they collected). They took away the keys, so others would open and close the meeting space, and when I was out of town, they offered to take turns leading the group. They wanted me to show up whenever I could and be a Zen teacher.

I was surprised, moved, and happy with this turn of events. For me, it was a big aha moment. Without any thought, I had done everything to run and manage this group. I was unaware of my resistance to depending on others and how this had stifled the growth of the group. Through my own sense of independence, I had, not very consciously, undermined the commitment of its members. Part of the dynamic was the habit we often fall into of thinking we have to do things by ourselves. And partly I had let fear — my fear of being let down and disappointed by others — keep me from letting go of control.

Mill Valley Zen, as a community, was born that evening. It went from being *my* group to *our* group. This shift from my not depending on others to depending on others transformed these relationships and transformed the Mill Valley Zen community.

A very similar dynamic and pattern is also at play in how we parent and how we lead. Looking back and reflecting on when my children were young, I had a tendency to do too much for them and not expect enough of them. Once I stopped waking them up in the morning and expected that they take responsibility for getting up, this supported their own sense of responsibility. The same was true for making school lunches each morning and a variety of other daily activities. When my children were older and finding their way in the world, I again had a strong tendency to want to support them. My reminder to myself in relationship to my children became: "I support them to be self-sufficient." This actually helped me a good deal, clarifying a way to be caring and to support their growth.

As a leader, I still can struggle with this tendency to go it alone and do for others rather than foster interdependence, collaboration, and shared responsibility. This is another important benefit of this practice: By letting go of our "need" to be independent, and letting ourselves depend on others, we empower others and help create a self-supportive community.

TRY THIS: Do a brief audit of the people who depend on you. Acknowledge and write about the ways that others depend on you. At the same time, notice and reflect on how you depend on others.

Let yourself sink into and fully embrace the mutual support you've given and received. Let yourself feel safe and held by other people in your life, and acknowledge the ways you've given this to others. In your journal, reflect on the meaning and richness this has provided. No one is perfect; others have sometimes let you down, and at times you've done the same. No matter. For now, fully appreciate your most important relationships, whatever role they play in your life.

TEAM BUILDING MEANS UNDERSTANDING WORK STYLES

In any group or community endeavor, but particularly at work, it's very helpful to understand everyone's strengths, weaknesses, and tendencies. This allows us to build strong teams despite our individual preferences and limitations, which is an important aspect of teamwork.

Obviously, this starts with yourself: What is your leadership or work style? Are you aware that you have a style? Review the four categories of work styles below. Which one, or which combination, comes closest to describing you? Of course, we are all capable of embodying any of these categories, depending on the context and needs, but in general, which one do you tend toward? Which is your predominant style?

- **THE VISIONARY:** You are someone who has an active imagination, lots of ideas, often big ideas, and you like others to gather around your vision. Having and driving toward a vision provides you with a good deal of energy.
- **THE ORGANIZER:** You love keeping things in order; you enjoy process, creating systems, and

keeping track of things. Overseeing or being part of organizing, tracking, and creating systems is energizing for you.

- **THE PEOPLE PERSON:** Your primary focus is on people — working with others, understanding others, and helping others. You get a good deal of energy and satisfaction from being with people.
- **THE DOER:** You orient around getting things done. You love marking things off your to-do lists, completing projects, and starting new ones.

Once you've identified your predominant style, try answering these questions in your journal:

1. What is special and important about your role?
2. What do you want the other roles to know about what you do and achieve?
3. How do you think your role is misunderstood or not fully appreciated by the other roles?

The point of this exercise is less to define yourself as a type than to reflect on four essential viewpoints that any organization needs in order to function. Every organization needs these four different perspectives, yet few people excel at and enjoy all four equally. Each viewpoint fulfills an important purpose, and many groups assign people to take on these responsibilities as their role, whether formally as part of a job title or informally as part of the group's collective expectation. Visionaries want to take the organization toward a large and noble purpose, and organizers depend on visionaries to provide a goal for their efforts. Then, without systems, visionaries would lead the organization toward chaos. All groups involve negotiation, compromise, and collaboration, so you also need people who are comfortable facilitating agreements and managing conflict, or nothing will get done at all. Finally, you need people who like to get their hands dirty and do what needs to be done, in addition to thinking, talking, and strategizing.

TRY THIS: Think of a group you work with, at work, in your community, or in your family. Consider what "type" of work style each person has; you can come up with your own categories if you wish. Then consider whether this group is balanced and complete. Is every necessary role accounted for? What skills might be lacking?

COLLABORATION MEANS UNDERSTANDING NORMS

There are many reasons for the recent upsurge of interest in mindfulness in the business world. One main reason, I believe, is the recognition that there is a strong correlation between success and creativity and the ability of employees to collaborate — to trust and support one another effectively in teams. A Google engineering manager once told me that while it's important to have really smart people on his team, what's even more important is the way in which the team interacts, trusts one another, and finds healthy ways to deal with conflict. Cultivating interdependence is what allows the team to find solutions and produce results. This is, of course, the same lesson I learned in the Zen kitchen, where mindfulness practice — developing self-awareness and cultivating an attitude of curiosity and generosity — is regarded as the key component of successful collaboration.

And *collaboration* is the current watchword in business.

In the January/February 2016 issue of *Harvard Business Review*, an article entitled "Collaborative Overload" begins with these observations and statistics:

> Collaboration is taking over the workplace. As business becomes increasingly global and cross-functional, silos are breaking down, connectivity is increasing, and teamwork is seen as a key to organizational success. According to data we have collected over the past two decades, the time spent by managers and employees in collaborative activities has ballooned by 50% or more.

In 2012, a few years after confirming the importance of good leaders, Google embarked on another research initiative, called Project Aristotle. They wanted to know why some teams underperformed, some were average performers, and others worked exceedingly well. Through research and massive data collection, they wanted to understand what makes the perfect team. Over a period of more than a year they looked at data and interviewed members from 180 different teams from various parts of the company, looking for patterns.

They were at first baffled. Despite all the data they were collecting, it was yielding very little information that helped them understand what differentiated groups. They weren't sure whether they were asking the right questions. Then, through their interview process, they discovered what they began to call the *norms* of people working together. Norms are agreements or unwritten rules that establish expectations and behavioral standards that govern how people interact. These norms are the ground truth; they define how people actually behave as opposed to the way they aspire to or say they want to behave. Norms define a company's culture and, ultimately, these norms determine the levels of trust, vulnerability, and functioning of teams. However, norms can vary among groups; each group might establish its own norms, which might differ (in ways large and small) from the norms of the organization overall.

In the Zen kitchen, mindfulness practice influenced the norms because we were Zen students in a Zen monastery. As a matter of course, we paid attention to how well groups functioned to support the kitchen's goals and the well-being of each person. This involved what I think of as "presence" and "embodiment" — evaluating the alignment of a person's words, values, heart, body language, and behavior; how much each person communicates real care and concern; how open each person is to feedback; and the level of each person's vulnerability.

Mindfulness practice does *not* generally influence the norms in most corporations and businesses today, and that's an important reason why mindful leadership is essential. Through our own example and efforts, we can help establish a norm of mindfulness that improves how groups collaborate and interact to get things done. We can use the seven practices to help foster the norms of high-performing teams Google identified through Project Aristotle. Google's final report stated that these positive norms include psychological safety, structure and clarity, dependability, meaning, and impact.

PSYCHOLOGICAL SAFETY: Team members developed a high level of trust and vulnerability. No one person dominated the discussions; everyone on the team spoke roughly the same amount of time during discussions. Team members showed a high level of emotional intelligence as measured by the ability to read facial expressions.

In a sense, any and all mindfulness practice is a tool for

developing greater psychological safety. At work, this means that each person on the team is open, curious, and vulnerable. They are engaged in the practices of not being an expert, connecting to their own pain, and connecting to the pain of others.

STRUCTURE AND CLARITY: High-performing teams exhibited clear goals and clear roles for team members. This was something that was done really well in the Zen monastery kitchen: we set clear goals and gave concrete assignments. It seems obvious but is often not given the attention it deserves — the importance of each person knowing exactly what success looks like for them, for their team, and for the organization.

DEPENDABILITY: Agreements were honored, and communication was clear about deadlines and expectations. My experience, such as with the open-leave policy at SIYLI, is that this requires putting regular systems into place regarding reports, measures, and feedback.

MEANING: The work the team was doing had some personal significance for each member. Identifying what's meaningful is an ongoing process for the leader and for all team members, and it requires regular storytelling about aspirations and about successes and failures. For the leader, this means inspiring others, whether they are cooking meals or coding a search engine. It also means focusing on the personal growth and well-being of each member as part of the team's mandate.

IMPACT: The work of the team was purposeful and seen as contributing to a positive impact. Impact can be experienced on a variety of levels: how working together improves the well-being of each team member and of the team as a whole, how the team is impacting the division or company, and how the organization impacts its customers and society.

TRY THIS: At work, how does your team compare on each of these categories: psychological safety, structure and clarity, dependability, meaning, and impact? Where are you doing well and where does your team need more attention? What changes and adjustments might you and your team make to support and increase successful collaboration?

MEETINGS: MINDFUL LEADERSHIP IN ACTION

Ah, meetings! Whenever I mention meetings, people often either roll their eyes or start to sweat a little. At every level at nearly every company I've ever worked with, people rarely hesitate to express disdain for meetings: "Too many meetings. I can't get my work done!"

I love meetings! That is, I love meetings that are well planned, well executed, and treated as a vital part of the group's functioning. Meetings are essential to forging great working relationships, to sharing information, and to solving problems. They are where the group manages the work of being a successful group, and where the group plans for and organizes what needs to be executed. They are where the positive culture of collaboration gets cultivated and embodied. This was one of my lessons in the Zen kitchen: Meetings provide opportunities for mindfulness that can be hard to find in the heat of working together, and when mindfulness flourishes in meetings, it shows up in the work everyone does together.

To me, the quickest and most sustainable way to shift a company culture is to change the way meetings are held. I firmly believe this, and I've expressed it to thousands of business leaders around the world. It really doesn't matter what companies do or produce: If you want to shift or improve organizational culture, focus on the way leaders run meetings.

Or, you might say, the one activity that requires the participation of everyone in the group, and the one activity in which everyone has an equal stake in the outcome, is when the group meets to coordinate how the group will function, decides what needs to be done, and evaluates how well previous work has gone. On a practical level, meetings are usually where the group's norms are established, and if mindful leaders are trying to cultivate a collaborative, cooperative, and supportive environment, meetings are the place to do it. They are an important place to practice "depend on others."

When meetings accomplish what they are intended to accomplish, they become vital tools for a number of purposes. And the first decision to make is to clarify what type of meeting you are having. Meetings can serve a variety of goals:

- **TEAM BUILDING:** Meetings can focus on fostering connection and building trust.
- **INFORMATION SHARING:** Meetings can be held to better understand who is doing what (or perhaps how they are working) to identify problems and opportunities for success.
- **PROBLEM SOLVING:** Meetings can focus on finding solutions to specific, ongoing challenges.

- **BRAINSTORMING:** By mining the wisdom of the group, meetings can open up unseen possibilities.
- **PLANNING AND COORDINATING:** Many meetings involve coordinating upcoming work by setting clear timelines and goals and clarifying who is doing what by when.
- **COMMUNICATION:** If people aren't communicating well, or the group isn't collaborating successfully, meetings can address how the group is functioning, as well as specific communication issues as they arise.

Of course, no single meeting should try to accomplish all of these objectives, but this list includes key reasons to meet. Without this preparation, the work itself can't be accomplished in the successful way every business and organization needs. Further, each objective requires a high level of mindfulness practice — incorporating, practicing, and embodying all of these seven practices.

How to Organize a Meeting

To me, successful meetings have two main components: norms and execution. The mindful leader's presence, behavior, and attitude helps cultivate the positive team attributes described in Google's Project Aristotle. These norms, especially psychological safety, are important factors not only for high-performing teams but for high-performing meetings. Without these norms, execution is irrelevant. Then again, well-structured, well-run meetings with a clear, meaningful purpose are what help build these healthy norms. When everyone expects meetings to be positive and productive, they arrive in a positive, productive frame of mind, which is obviously ideal for getting things done.

Successful meeting execution depends on three things: preparation, running the meeting, and follow-up.

MEETING PREPARATION: Before calling a meeting, clarify for yourself and others the purpose of the meeting, the type of meeting it will be, who should attend, and the agenda. A good test for clarifying the purpose of a meeting is to envision the intended outcome. Ideally, what will result from this meeting?

Then decide the type of meeting, using the list above as a guide. Will this be a meeting for team building, brainstorming, or problem solving? Experiment with different types of meetings, as needs arise. Avoid the pattern or habit of having the same type of meeting week after week (unless, of course, having the same meeting is necessary, compelling, alive, and useful for all involved). I've seen many teams get into the rut of having all meetings be about reporting what each person is doing. This can be useful at times, but not always, and it's just one type of or purpose for having a meeting.

A critical and often overlooked aspect of meetings is deciding who should and who should not attend. Pay attention to having the right people and the right number of people to achieve the intended goals. Also important is deciding how often to meet. Experiment. I've seen teams shift from meeting once a week to once a month, and other teams discovered they needed to meet more often than they were.

Finally, another obvious and often overlooked aspect of well-executed meetings is the agenda. What's the plan and what are the priorities? How much time is being allocated to each part of the meeting? Be specific, and let people know the agenda, so they can come prepared.

RUNNING THE MEETING: Transitions are important, so open and close meetings in ways that encourage presence and focus. When possible, I suggest starting with silence. Even thirty seconds or a minute of sitting quietly can focus and settle the room's energy and encourage mindfulness. When possible, I suggest creating some kind of check-in where everyone gets to speak and express what's going on for them (separately from the meeting's agenda), even if it is only one or two words.

Then, close the meeting in a similar way. Just as opening a meeting is important to the meeting's success, the way a meeting ends also matters. I like to hear from everyone in the meeting again, even if it is just one word, or to end with another brief period of silence. Experiment to find simple opening and closing rituals that foster mindful awareness and create a sense of safety, connection, and care.

As for the meeting itself, ensure that someone is responsible for facilitating the discussion and keeping the group focused and on track, so that the meeting flows and stays aligned with the agenda. The facilitator is not necessarily the leader but another designated group member. Skilled facilitation means mindful facilitation — keeping an eye on the energy, feelings, and emotions of the group, managing any conflict and disagreement, and making sure the discussion addresses what it's meant to.

Once it's time to end the meeting, and before any closing ritual, summarize the outcome and any action items. Be explicit and share with the group what has been decided and what remains to be decided. Be clear about who is doing what by a specific date.

FOLLOW-UP: I generally suggest following up meetings with a group communication that names the action items that resulted and the next steps. This isn't a review of the entire meeting, like sharing the minutes, but a reminder and summary of what needs to be done and who needs to do it. This is essential so that meetings are part of the ongoing development of projects and moving toward achieving overall goals and vision.

GOOD MEETINGS EMBODY A MINDFUL CULTURE

Experiment and explore how to make meetings work in your company, work environment, or group. Preparing for meetings takes time, but in my experience, it is well worth it. Good meetings embody the mindful culture that leads to success for any business and all involved.

For example, Plantronics is a publicly traded company in Santa Cruz, California, that was one of the first companies to participate in the Search Inside Yourself mindfulness-based emotional intelligence training outside of Google. And one of the main changes they made was how they conducted meetings, which led to significant positive results.

At that time the SIY training met each week for seven weeks. At Plantronics, the participants were the top fifty leaders and managers of the company, including the CEO and the head of human resources. Over these weeks, we were able to create a safe and caring space. Many participants reported that, despite working together for ten or even twenty years or more, they had rarely or never spoken with one another in ways that were vulnerable, open, and fostered a spirit of trust and connection.

The impact of this was immediate and often quantifiable. After the seven-week training, the company reported that their meetings were much more focused and productive. They were accomplishing more in less time, which resulted in a significant cost savings. Leadership also said that employee morale improved, meaning that the company was achieving more and becoming a better place to work, in large part because they were improving their meetings. Not all the changes were the result of meetings, but it never fails to strike me how relevant and impactful mindfulness practice can be.

TRY THIS: Evaluate the meetings where you work. Whatever your role, how might you incorporate mindfulness and help meetings function better? Ask yourself the following questions.

Is the purpose of each meeting clear? If not, how might you help clarify the purpose?

Are all meetings the same type? How might you vary the types of meetings so each aligns with its purpose?

Do you and your team look forward to meetings? If not, what steps can you take to improve expectations and the experience of meetings?

What are the cultural and behavioral norms in your workplace and in your meetings? What is the level of trust, vulnerability, and joy? What stands in the way of these?

How might you use and integrate mindfulness practices with your meetings to improve any and all of these aspects?

DEPEND ON OTHERS

KEY PRACTICES

- In your role as a leader, explore and focus on coaching, empowering, and listening to others.
- Notice your resistance to depending on others and embrace interdependence.
- Meditate with and for others to help develop a regular meditation practice.
- Do a brief audit: Who depends on you? And how do you depend on others?
- Consider your work style — visionary, organizer, people person, or doer — and the work styles of others when building a group or team.
- Seek to cultivate positive group norms of psychological safety, structure and clarity, dependability, meaning, and impact.
- As necessary, change the way meetings are conducted to foster mindfulness and a collaborative, cooperative, supportive environment.

PART THREE

INTEGRATE

PRACTICE 7

KEEP MAKING IT SIMPLER

Traveler, there is no path.
You make your own path with each step you take.
— Antonio Machado

Whenever I lead trainings or give talks on using these seven mindfulness practices, I can often feel the room's energy shift as I describe the seventh practice, "Keep making it simpler." People experience a sense of relief, as though a weight has been lifted. Their shoulders drop and they relax. Though we yearn for and need practices to support our leadership, mindfulness, and growth, we also have a basic and primal yearning to let go, to let it all go — all our concerns and judgments about our health, well-being, improvement, effort, and struggles over everything, including these practices. What a relief to stop struggling!

Imagine, for just a short amount of time each day, letting go of your to-do lists, your self-help plans, and your projects. Imagine letting go of your improvement plans for others. This is often really difficult. Each day, just appreciate this moment, your life right now as it is.

In meditation practice we train our minds to be aware, to be with whatever sensations, feelings, and thoughts arise. A somewhat radical-sounding practice is to let go of everything with each exhale, to not assume or expect that your exhale will be followed by another inhale. With each breath, let go even of the expectation of being alive. Then, when there is another inhale, be surprised: *Oh, here I am!*

Acceptance — embracing the fact of impermanence and the certainty of change — is a powerful tool for cultivating simplicity. Much of our doing is extra and moves us in the direction of complexity. The key is to integrate doing and non-doing, effort and effortlessness. This isn't some magic trick or ancient, mysterious spiritual practice. When you are speaking or writing, just speak or write, without doing anything extra. This same attitude of just doing what you are doing (without comparing or judging or trying to get to the next activity) can be cultivated in leading, in listening, in driving, in working alone or with others, in relationships, as well as in your daily activities.

The intention of the seventh practice is to see or recognize the most important thing in any given moment, even in the midst of our busy lives. We can't avoid challenges, or problems, or grief, or death, but when we feel confused and overwhelmed, we can remember: Keep making it simpler, and simpler still; each moment and each day, keep making life less complicated, so we are more focused, spacious, and present. So we prioritize the most important action to take.

THE EIGHTY-FOURTH PROBLEM

Once upon a time, during the life of the historical Buddha, there was a farmer who had many problems. He had heard about the

Buddha's great wisdom and decided to ask the Buddha directly for help.

His list of complaints was long. The weather was either too dry or too wet, and his crops were always less abundant than expected. Though he loved his wife, she was at times critical and sharp. He was disappointed with his children. As they had grown, they had become less appreciative of him. His neighbors often interfered in his life and spread false rumors about him.

The Buddha looked at him and said that unfortunately he couldn't help the farmer with any of his problems. He said, "All human beings have eighty-three problems. That's just the way life is. When you solve one problem, another appears and takes its place. My teaching can't help you with your problems, but perhaps my teaching can help you with the eighty-fourth problem."

"What is the eighty-fourth problem?" asked the farmer.

"The eighty-fourth problem is that you don't want to have any problems," the Buddha said.

A key aspect of "keep making it simpler" is training the body and mind to let go of resisting what is and of striving for what isn't. The Buddha doesn't tell the farmer that he doesn't have problems. Everyone has problems. In fact, according to Buddha, everyone has exactly eighty-three problems, no more and no less. Problems are part of being human, part of our common humanity. Rather, Buddha suggests that the farmer is not alone in his predicament, and that he wants something no one can have. This is his eighty-fourth problem, the only problem that Buddha can help with.

The Buddha teaches that once you stop trying to make your problems go away, you and your problems are transformed and your problems aren't what you thought. They are not separate from your life. Your "problems" are the richness and texture of being human. You can own that you want things to be different and face your problems directly, without judgment or resistance. When you do this, you are more able to meet and transform whatever problems arise. We all want to become more effective at work, to improve communication with our partner and our children, and to establish better relationships. But that work is never ending, never over. Success never results in fewer problems. With this practice, we simplify our life through our approach and attitude, without expecting anything else.

TRY THIS: Explore practicing greater acceptance. This doesn't mean ignoring your pain, problems, and difficulties. It means that, for right now, you accept them completely without trying to change them or make anything different. How? Call to mind a particular difficult situation that is part of your life right now. Experiment with these three steps.

1. **TURN TOWARD THE DIFFICULTY** — face it and see it head on.
2. **ACCEPT** — allow yourself to see and feel the pain of this difficult situation; this takes courage, and mindfulness practice helps.
3. **LET GO OF BLAME** — this includes yourself and others.

BE BOTH RELAXED AND ALERT

When teaching meditation practice, my initial instructions for participants generally start: "Find a way to sit in your chair where you can be both relaxed and alert." I then add: "This practice, this way of being, isn't preparing to meditate. This is a core aspect of the practice — training your body and mind to be both relaxed and alert at the same time."

This is what athletes work to achieve, whether pitching a baseball, hitting a golf shot in a major tournament, or serving in an important tennis match. When it matters, you want to be as relaxed and alert as possible. This is what I aim for when leading a staff meeting or giving a keynote talk. I want to be fully comfortable, open, at ease, and I want to be aware, awake, ready to meet each situation fully. Too relaxed and I may be unaware or sleepy; too alert and I'm at risk of overreacting, of being tense or not fully present.

TRY THIS: Right now, explore being relaxed and alert at the same time. To relax, bring your attention to the breath. Breathe fully in and out. To be alert, bring your attention to your body. Open your shoulders and arch your spine slightly. Do this whenever you think of it during the day.

MEDITATION: LETTING GO OF EXTRA EFFORT

When I'm leading meditations, after guiding people to find that relaxed and alert state, I then suggest letting it all go: Let go of trying, of unnecessary effort, and just notice what comes to you. This is an important part of all the seven practices: Noticing and letting go of extra effort, of resisting your problems, of resisting change, of trying to change, and instead embrace your life as it is.

Imagine: What would your life be like if you had a different relationship with your problems, if you could completely accept and be at peace with your problems? The meditation that follows explores understanding and working with the eighty-fourth problem, that of wanting not to have problems.

To begin, notice that you are breathing. Simply bring your attention to your breath, sometimes inhaling and sometimes exhaling. As you exhale, notice that you are exhaling, and see if you can let go of all your problems, everything.

Simply bring your attention to your breath. Breathing in and breathing out.

Then, for the length of one long, full exhale, let go:

Let go of your to-do lists, unfinished projects, and anything that is lacking or needs to be improved or fixed.

Let go of all your self-help plans, and even more difficult for many, let go of your self-help plans for others.

Let go of doing or thinking that is extra or unnecessary right now.

Imagine: What might it feel like to appreciate your problems and let go of resisting them?

Then, as you inhale, let all your problems, lists, and issues resurface. Then, with the next exhale, let them go.

Continue for as long as feels comfortable, and when you are ready, bring your attention back to your surroundings and gently reenter your day.

DON'T BE BUSY — BE FOCUSED, ENGAGED, AND SPACIOUS

"Are you as busy as we are?"

This was the question a female executive from a technology company once asked me as we began our Skype meeting.

I was talking with her regarding the Search Inside Yourself Leadership Institute, and I could have easily said yes. Instead I said, "We don't do busy. We aspire to work in a way that is focused, engaged, and spacious."

I was attempting to be playful, and we both laughed. Of course I was busy, but I have a strong aversion to busyness, and she and I then had a meaningful discussion about our intention for how we wanted to work. It's easy to get caught up in the prevailing culture of busyness. Having a lot to do is one thing; it's a common problem we are all familiar with. To me, busyness means becoming caught up in that complexity and losing sight of what is most important. Busyness equates to mindless rushing. For me, the antidote to busyness is remembering to be mindful and to practice being focused, engaged, and spacious.

What does this mean?

FOCUSED: See what matters most, your ground truth, your creative gap, the most important thing, and focus on that. Come back, over and over, to the simple, yet difficult question: *What is my priority right now? What is the most important thing to accomplish in this call, this day, this week?*

ENGAGED: This refers to your level of energy and attention. Whatever the task, engage with it fully till it's time to move to a new task. In general, I find I can remain fully engaged with tasks in forty-five- to ninety-minute increments, then it helps to take a short break of five or ten minutes. When working, engage with your full energy, then completely disengage and relax.

SPACIOUS: This refers to bringing your attention away from concerns about yourself and noticing the space and openness, literally, that exists around you, wherever you are. At the same time, notice stress without becoming stressed. Expect stress, anxiety, and fear to arise at times, and let them go when they do. Studies show that stress and busyness aren't the real problem; the problem is our relationship with stress. In one study, people who believed that stress was inevitable and positive had greater well-being than those who believed that stress was negative and something to be avoided. Further, those who had a positive attitude about stress lived longer than those who experienced relatively little stress in their lives.

TRY THIS: Right now, notice where you may be feeling tight or constricted. Give attention to those places, and relax and soften them. Notice how much space is now available. So often we miss how much space there is right in the midst of our busy lives. We tend to look only at people and things and miss how much space there is in between. Explore, notice how much space there is, physically. Right now, look up, look to the left and right. There is lots of space everywhere. Then return to the question of what matters most to you right now.

Making it simpler doesn't mean avoiding stress or accomplishing less. There is a good deal of evidence that we can live healthier lives and accomplish more, and more of what matters, when we are focused, engaged, and spacious.

SIMPLIFY DECISIONS BY CREATING ROUTINES

Children love routines, as do adults. Routines free our minds from decision-making and complexity, especially healthy routines that are in alignment with what matters most.

I love and depend on my morning routine, as well as

routines throughout my day. I'm up each day at 5:30 AM. Wash up, some light yoga, and then twenty minutes of mindfulness meditation. From 6:30 to 7:00 AM, I read, starting with a book, then moving to the *New York Times*. I have breakfast at 7:00 AM. After lunch I take a fifteen- to twenty-minute nap, often in my car, but when that's not possible, I can usually find a quiet, out-of-the-way place. Late in the afternoon I go for a walk, from thirty to sixty minutes. When possible, I walk in the hills above the Pacific Ocean north of San Francisco. My default walk is on the streets in my Mill Valley neighborhood. I'm in bed by 10:30 PM, reading until about 11:00.

When people tell me they have a difficult time establishing a meditation practice, I suggest they treat it like the routine of brushing your teeth. We don't need to decide each morning whether to brush our teeth or not. I don't need to decide about meditating each morning. Simple.

Consider right now: What are your routines? What healthy routines might you create and install in your life?

RETREATS: TAKE BIG BREAKS

Regular silent mindfulness meditation retreats are an important way to support making your life simpler. What could be simpler than just being quiet, sitting, with nothing to do or accomplish for days at a time? This is *the* core practice of simplicity.

If you have never done a five-to-seven-day mindfulness meditation retreat, I highly recommend it. I understand that taking this kind of time off can be difficult; it may not be possible for everyone. If you have done a long retreat, see if you can get in the habit of doing one each year.

My ideal retreat schedule is to do a half-day or full-day

retreat each month and a five-to-seven-day retreat each year. There are many forms of retreats in addition to mindfulness meditation retreats. Explore a yoga retreat or walking or camping in the wilderness, either by yourself or with a group. The point is to step out of the intensity and the busyness of life, making time to simplify. Then, when returning to your usual activities, to integrate simplicity with the demands of daily life.

YOU HAVE ONLY ONE PRIORITY

Several years ago I attended a weeklong Art of Leadership training led by Robert Gass. Robert stood in front of a group of twenty CEOs of socially responsible companies, next to a flip chart with a large sheet of blank white paper. He asked the group, "What is it we have no choice about in our lives? What must we do?" At first, I and the group were startled, wondering what the point of this exercise was. "Eating" someone suggested, and Robert put this on the sheet of paper. "Working" someone suggested. Robert responded that working is a choice. You could not work, and if you live in Canada (where the workshop was being held) or the United States (and most parts of the world), you would be fed and taken care of in some way. Thus working is a choice. The point of the exercise was to recognize and see clearly that nearly everything we do is a choice. Once we realize that we have more choices than we usually think, the next task becomes to prioritize.

Greg McKeown points out in the book *Essentialism* that the word *priority* came into use in the English language in the 1400s. It meant the first thing or the prior thing. It was singular. Five hundred years later, in the 1900s, the word became plural, from *priority* to *priorities*. McKeown writes, "Illogically we reasoned that by changing the word we could bend reality. Somehow we would now be able to have multiple first things."

In fact, we have to choose what one thing takes priority in every moment, and we have the power to choose. This may sound obvious, but let it sink in for a moment. It's easy to forget. Powerfully, surprisingly, in every moment you are choosing, deciding how to respond appropriately, deciding how to spend your time, your energy, your attention. If you don't prioritize your life, someone else will.

My first job after getting my MBA degree was with a small recycled paper distributor, Conservatree Paper Company in San Francisco. I had two small children at home, and I found it difficult to be away from them each day. Further, Conservatree's culture, part of its norms or unwritten assumptions, included an expectation that people would work late into the evening. During my first few weeks, I made a choice: I told my boss that I needed to leave the office by 5:00 PM every night so I could have dinner with my family. I felt anxious making this request. I was telling my employer that they were not the most important thing all the time. However, I found that being clear about my priorities was respected, and leaving at 5:00 PM was rarely a problem.

YOU HAVE ONLY ONE CAREER

Since I work in the corporate world, I find I am frequently asked for career advice. I'm struck by how many people are in transition in their work. Nearly everyone is subject to the rapid changes in technology and to corporate and economic upheaval in general — doing more with less resources, the expectation to be on call 24/7, the increase in the pace and complexity of work, and how common it is to work virtually and globally. Each one of these factors increases the complexity of our work lives. Together, they add up to a tremendous challenge. Add the full catastrophe of our personal lives, and it's never easy to foster calm, meaning, connection with others, and a life of health and well-being.

My suggestion is to explore thinking differently about the true nature of your career. I believe we all have only one career. It's a career that spans and integrates work, relationships, and all parts of our lives. This career is living a mindful life.

The twin goals of this career are to develop your awareness and to help others, and all other activities should serve these two goals. This is a powerful and effective way to move from complexity to simplicity. Perhaps not easy, but simple. What might your life be like if you approach all activities from the perspective of this career? You might find that busyness and complexity greatly diminish. Complexity doesn't disappear — you are complex, life is complex, your work is probably complex. Activity doesn't disappear — you will still have to juggle many needs, desires, and sometimes competing priorities. Yet developing your awareness and helping others is simple.

Developing your awareness is the essence of mindfulness practice. It means remembering to pause in the midst of movement and change. To stay with your breathing, to bring awareness to your body, to your feelings, intuition, and heart. Sometimes focusing, sometimes expanding, sweeping, being curious. Asking yourself regularly: *What is most important right now?*

Helping others is leadership. It means noticing what is needed in a group, family, company, or community. It means noticing when others need assistance or attention and trying to provide it. It means cultivating empathy, listening, and being open to other people's experience, and looking for ways and opportunities to be of service. Leaders regularly ask: *How might I help?*

TO SIMPLIFY, TAKE THREE BREATHS

When you need to simplify, to clarify what is most important, try this three-breath practice.

- With the first breath, notice your body; just become aware of whatever is happening with your shoulders, back, stomach.
- With the second breath, notice your feelings; just become aware of whatever you are feeling right now.
- With the third breath, ask yourself, right now: *What's the most important thing?*

Three breaths. One body. One heart. One mind.
Simple.
Keep making it simpler.

KEEP MAKING IT SIMPLER

KEY PRACTICES

- Explore letting go of your to-do lists, plans, and projects, just for a few minutes each day.
- Practice greater acceptance. Experiment with turning toward difficulty, accepting it, and letting go of blame.

- During any activity, practice being alert and relaxed.
- Meditate to practice letting go of extra effort.
- Explore being more focused, engaged, and spacious as an antidote to busyness.
- Notice your routines and add new ones that foster mindfulness.
- Go on regular retreats.
- Consider that you have one career: cultivating awareness and helping others.
- In any moment, simplify using the three breaths practice: focus on body, breath, and what is most important.

EPILOGUE

I keep thinking that what we need is a new language... a language of the heart... a new kind of poetry that tells us where the honey is.... And I think that in order to create that language you're going to have to learn how to go through a looking glass into another kind of perception where you have that sense of being united to all things.... And suddenly you understand everything.

— Andre Gregory, *My Dinner with Andre*

The poet and writer David Whyte describes a time when he was giving a public poetry reading and was approached by a businessman who asked him if he would come to his company and read poetry. Until this time David had considered himself a somewhat traditional poet and writer. He asked, "Why would I do that?" The man responded, "My company needs what your words and message provide. They lift the human spirit, taking us from the ordinary and mundane to something larger than ourselves." This man was a senior leader at the Boeing Company.

My experience teaching mindfulness at Google and to companies and individuals around the world is that there is a tremendous need and hunger for understanding and developing greater humanness, openness, and inspiration, not only at work, but in all parts of our lives. Mindfulness practice is potent. It enables us to see more clearly and to engage with the miracle of consciousness, the miracle of being alive.

Mindfulness practice can shift the ground of our consciousness, our presence, our being — not by adding something, such as a new belief system, or by seeking inspiration, but by presenting a more accurate view of what is, of human nature and how we construct and constrict our version of ourselves and the world.

Mindfulness practice is aimed at understanding and shifting the nature of fear, dissatisfaction, and the experience of separateness. Mindfulness practice helps us glimpse how what we thought was ordinary is extraordinary, how mundane life is miraculous at the same time.

Why is mindful leadership and being a human being so difficult? Why does it take so much attention and effort to be present, to wake up to our lives, to discover again and again that we are not here long, and to pay attention to what is in our heart, to what is right here, to what is most obvious and most important right now?

Reflecting on this, I can't help but think about my friends, the three apes, who play a central metaphoric role in this book. They represent the evolution of our bodies, minds, and hearts and our primary needs for safety, satisfaction, and connection. Human beings did not evolve, were not designed, to see clearly but primarily to survive, to pass on our genes. Being a mindful leader requires effort because it requires letting go of old constructed realities, the norms that no longer serve us, our organizations, or our families. Living with clarity and depth, living a mindful, integrated, warmhearted life takes practice.

Aspiring to be a mindful leader and engaging in these seven practices helps calm the nervous ape's vigilance and fear (its proclivity to scan for threats); it satisfies the imaginative ape, who is always seeking something new and better; and it reassures the empathic ape that we are always connected, beyond anything we can comprehend. Engaging in mindfulness practice calls forth our basic sanity in the midst of a world that often feels chaotic. Mindfulness practice knocks on the door of our inborn openness and trust in a world that can often feel cold and cynical.

Considering why mindful leadership is so difficult and necessary, I also return to the themes of pain and possibility. This pain is the pain of change, of not getting what we want and of getting what we don't want. Opening to possibility shifts our relationship with desire itself, rather than striving to satisfy our desires (though that may happen). Our freedom lies in a radical acceptance of what is as well as in the power of awareness. Seeing inner freedom as possible is a core underlying aspect of mindfulness and mindful leadership.

"Everyone wants to leave the endless changes." This is a line from a sixth-century verse by Dongshan, the founder of the Soto Zen School in China. Time and change are beyond our usual, rational understanding. You are not alone in your resistance to change. Staying with the questions, staying with what is, takes courage. Notice what happens when you fully enter your life, your experience, with less resistance. And when resistance arises, great! Notice your resistance. It is a terrific teacher.

Later in the same verse, Dongshan says, "When we stop bending and fitting our lives, we come back to sit by the fire." What would it be like to pause, to stop bending and fitting your life, to not hold back? Then to sit, relaxed and alert, by the warmth of our innermost knowing, feeling the heat from the fire within and around us that always burns.

ACKNOWLEDGMENTS

"Depend on others" is practice 6. I've depended on others for every part of this book — during my time in the Tassajara kitchen, leading trainings at Google, as CEO of the Search Inside Yourself Leadership Institute, and including the full spectrum of my work and life, all of which has been poured into this effort.

I'll start with my years in the Tassajara kitchen. During my first summer as dishwasher, Steve Weintraub supported me in his role as head cook. During my first winter, Dana Dantine was the head cook and asked me to be on the kitchen crew and then to be the summer baker. A few years later I was assistant to the head cook while Teah Strozer ran the kitchen, and the following year when I was head cook, Gil Fronsdale was the assistant. While working in the kitchen, I learned a good deal from Meg Alexander, Chris Fortin, Richard Jaffe, Michael Gelfond, Karin Gjording, Annie Sommerville, and many others — cooking, baking, and practicing together.

Thank you to Mike Dixon for first bringing me into Google. You had no idea of the doors you opened. And to Chade-Meng Tan for inviting me to be part of the original Search Inside Yourself team. Punit Aggarwal, Dolores Bernardo, Hemant Bhanoo, Sudhakar Chandra, Bill Duane, Mario Galarreta, Jenny Lykken, Karen May, Liz Olson, Van Riper, Paul Santagata, Ruchika Sikri, and many others supported me at Google. Philippe Goldin's mentoring was invaluable.

Thank you to my Search Inside Yourself Leadership Institute colleagues, especially Kimiko Bokura, Peter Bonanno, Peter Bostelmann, Laurie Cameron, Mark Coleman, Linda Curtis, Rick Echler, Ilana Robbins Gross, Judith Harris, Caro Hart, Lindsey Kugel, Meg Levie, Nina Levit, Michelle Maldonado, Simon Moyes, Alex Moyle, Tyler Peterson, Brandon Rennels, Jason Sbordone, Lori Schwanbeck, Stephanie Stern, Peter Weng, and Regina Zasadzinski. And to the Search Inside Yourself community.

Much appreciation to Norman Fischer, good friend and esteemed dharma teacher — for your creativity and wisdom, and for bringing forth these seven practices. To Michael Wenger, my other root teacher, and to friend and teacher Paul Haller.

Thanks to my Social Venture Network Peer Circle for ongoing leadership support: Judi Cohen, Jay Harris, Elliot Hoffman, Aaron Lamstein, David Leventhal, Jared Levy, and Jill Portman.

Thanks to my Old Zen Guys for keeping my practice alive: Marc Alexander, Bruce Fortin, Michael Gelfond, Rick Levine, Ken Sawyer, Peter Van der Sterre, and Steve Weintraub.

Thank you to the "leadership team" of Mill Valley Zen: Judith James, Karen Lang, Loretta Lowrey, David Maxwell, and Dharna Obermaier for keeping it all together.

I appreciate my ongoing leadership and life conversations with Mitch Anthony, Deborah Berman, Martin Berman, Debra Dunn, Daniel Ellenberg, Bruce Feldman, Lori Hanau, Rick Hanson, Roger Housden, Craig Litman, Jackie McGrath, Richard Miller, Deborah Nelson, Dan Siegel, Lucinda Rhys, Peter Strugatz, and David Yeung.

Thank you to Jason Gardner of New World Library for believing in me and this book project through its many transitions and transformations. And much appreciation to Monique Muhlenkamp, Munro Magruder, and the New World Library team for terrific support.

Thank you to Jennifer Futernick for your early work in helping to shape this book.

I appreciate the writing feedback from Krista de Castella, Robyn Morris, Roger Asleson, Jay Harris, Vanessa Meade, Wendy Quan, Tina de Salvo, and Kelly Werner.

Thank you to Jeff Campbell, editor extraordinaire and thought partner, for pushing, pulling, and guiding me all along the way.

Doing bows of appreciation to my wife, Lee, for her relentless, wholehearted love, honesty, and support. And to my children, Jason and Carol, for enriching my life and helping me to keep my heart open.

Deep appreciation to my mother and father, Beatrice and Ralph Lesser, for providing unconditional love.

NOTES

INTRODUCTION

Page 7, *In an essay entitled "Instructions to the Head Cook"*: Kazuaki Tanahashi, ed., *Moon in a Dewdrop: Writings of Zen Master Dogen* (New York: North Point Press, 1985).

Page 21, *In the chapter "The Billion-Dollar Mistake," Goleman describes*: Daniel Goleman, *Working with Emotional Intelligence* (New York: Bantam Books, 1998), 235.

PRACTICE I: LOVE THE WORK

Page 37, *In* The Leadership Challenge, *a classic, bestselling leadership manual*: James Kouzes and Barry Posner, *The Leadership Challenge* (San Francisco: Jossey-Bass, 2012), 345.

Page 42, *For instance, a 2011 study entitled "How Does Mindfulness Meditation Work?"*: Britta Holzel et al., "How Does Mindfulness Meditation Work? Proposing Mechanisms of Action from a Conceptual and Neural Perspective," *Perspectives on Psychological Science* 6, no. 6 (October 14, 2011), doi:10.1177/1745691611419671.

Page 54, *In* Altered Traits, *Davidson and coauthor Daniel Goleman describe*: Daniel Goleman and Richard Davidson, *Altered Traits: Science Reveals How Meditation Changes Your Mind, Brain, and Body* (New York: Avery, 2017), 123.

PRACTICE 2: DO THE WORK

Page 61, *Here is what Dogen, founder of Zen in Japan in the thirteenth century*: Norman Waddell and Masao Abe, trans., *The Heart of Dogen's Shobogenzo* (Albany: State University of New York Press, 2002).

Page 70, *Otto Scharmer, a senior lecturer at MIT and author of* Leading from the Emerging Future: Otto Scharmer and Katrin Kaufer, *Leading from the Emerging Future* (San Francisco: Berrett-Koehler, 2013).

Page 73, *A series of studies conducted by Juliana Breines and Serena Chen*: Juliana Breines and Serena Chen, "Self-Compassion Increases Self-Improvement Motivation," *Personality and Social Psychology Bulletin* 38, no. 9 (May 29, 2012), doi:10.1177/0146167212445599.

PRACTICE 3: DON'T BE AN EXPERT

Page 93, *Some psychological research estimates that 10 percent of our actions*: Timothy Wilson, *Strangers to Ourselves: Discovering the Adaptive Unconscious* (Cambridge, MA: Belknap Press of Harvard University Press, 2004).

Page 93, *This automation process is said to have a neural basis*: H. H. Yin and B. J. Knowlton, "The Role of the Basal Ganglia in Habit Formation," *Nature Reviews Neuroscience* 7, no. 6 (June 2006): 464–76, doi:10.1038/nrn1919.

Page 93, *For example, here is an abstract summary of a scientific paper by Justin Brewer*: Justin Brewer et al., "Meditation Experience Is Associated with Differences in Default Mode Network Activity and

Connectivity," *Proceedings of the National Association of Science* 108, no. 50 (November 22, 2011), doi:10.1073/pnas.1112029108.

Page 95, *"The two selves are the experiencing self, which does the living"*: Daniel Kahneman, *Thinking, Fast and Slow* (New York: Farrar, Straus and Giroux, 2011), 408–9.

Page 97, *"I cannot experience your experience"*: R. D. Laing, *The Politics of Experience* (New York: Ballantine Books, 1971).

PRACTICE 4: CONNECT TO YOUR PAIN

Page 110, *In the West, this discovery was expressed by the Roman emperor*: Marcus Aurelius, *Meditations* (Mineola, NY: Dover Publications, 1997).

PRACTICE 5: CONNECT TO THE PAIN OF OTHERS

Page 126, *there is some evidence that greater leadership authority is correlated*: Lou Solomon, "Becoming Powerful Makes You Less Empathetic," *Harvard Business Review*, April 21, 2015.

Page 127, *Dr. John Gottman studies the factors that lead married couples*: Ellie Lisitsa, "The Four Horsemen: The Antidotes," Gottman Institute, April 26, 2013, https://www.gottman.com/blog/the-four-horsemen-the-antidotes.

Page 139, *The video features a young woman singing "The Star-Spangled Banner"*: "Mo Cheeks National Anthem," YouTube, posted August 8, 2006, https://www.youtube.com/watch?v=q4880PJnO2E.

PRACTICE 6: DEPEND ON OTHERS

Page 146, *in 2008, they decided to conduct a study called Google Oxygen*: Melissa Harrell and Lauren Barbato, "Great Managers Still Matter: The Evolution of Google's Project Oxygen," re:Work,

February 27, 2018, https://rework.withgoogle.com/blog/the-evolution-of-project-oxygen.

Page 161, *In the January/February 2016 issue of* Harvard Business Review, *an article*: Rob Cross, Reb Rebele, and Adam Grant, "Collaborative Overload," *Harvard Business Review* (January/February 2016).

Page 161, *Google embarked on another research initiative, called Project Aristotle*: "Guide: Understand Team Effectiveness, https://rework.withgoogle.com/guides/understanding-team-effectiveness/steps/introduction.

PRACTICE 7: KEEP MAKING IT SIMPLER

Page 182, *In one study, people who believed that stress was inevitable*: Kelly McGonigal, *The Upside of Stress* (New York: Avery, 2015).

Page 184, *Greg McKeown points out in the book* Essentialism *that*: Greg McKeown, *Essentialism: The Disciplined Pursuit of Less* (New York: Crown Business, 2014).

EPILOGUE

Page 189, *The poet and writer David Whyte describes a time when he was giving*: David Whyte, *Clear Mind, Wild Heart: Finding Courage and Clarity through Poetry*, Sounds True, 2002, CD.

Page 191, *"Everyone wants to leave the endless changes"*: This verse by Dongshan is quoted from John Tarrant, "Method of Decision," KALPA, July 6, 2017, https://www.pacificzen.org/library/method-of-decision.

RECOMMENDED READING

This recommended reading section combines books on leadership, mindfulness, science, the humanities, and an occasional novel. What connects them is the attempt to make sense of human beings and the world we live in. These are among the books I find myself regularly suggesting to my friends and clients:

Burdick, Alan. *Why Time Flies: A Mostly Scientific Investigation*. New York: Simon & Schuster, 2017.

D'Ansembourg, Thomas. *Being Genuine: Stop Being Nice, Start Being Real*. Encinitas, CA: PuddleDancer Press, 2007.

Goleman, Daniel, and Richard Davidson. *Altered Traits: Science Reveals How Meditation Changes Your Mind, Brain, and Body*. New York: Avery, 2017.

Hanson, Rick, and Forrest Hanson. *Resilient: How to Grow an Unshakable Core of Calm, Strength, and Happiness*. New York: Harmony, 2018.

Harari, Yuval Noah. *Sapiens: A Brief History of Humankind*. New York: HarperCollins, 2015.

———. *Homo Deus: A Brief History of Tomorrow*. New York: HarperCollins, 2017.

Hougaard, Rasmus, and Jacqueline Carter. *The Mind of the Leader: How to Lead Yourself, Your People, and Your Organization for Extraordinary Results*. Boston: Harvard Business Review Press, 2018.

Kahane, Adam. *Power and Love: A Theory and Practice of Social Change*. San Francisco: Berrett-Koehler Publishers, 2010.

Kahneman, Daniel. *Thinking Fast and Slow*. New York: Farrar, Straus and Giroux, 2011.

McCullough, David. *The Wright Brothers*. New York: Simon & Schuster, 2015.

Ostaseski, Frank. *The Five Invitations: Discovering What Death Can Teach Us About Living Fully*. New York: Flatiron Books, 2017.

Ozeki, Ruth. *A Tale for the Time Being: A Novel*. New York: Penguin Books, 2013.

Pinker, Steven. *Enlightenment Now: The Case for Reason, Science, Humanism, and Progress*. New York: Viking, 2018.

Pollan, Michael. *How To Change Your Mind: What the New Science of Psychedelics Teaches Us About Consciousness, Dying, Addiction, Depression, and Transcendence*. New York: Penguin Press, 2018.

Siegel, Daniel. *Aware: The Science and Practice of Presence*. New York: TarcherPerigee, 2018.

Sinek, Simon. *Leaders Eat Last: Why Some Teams Pull Together and Others Don't*. New York: Portfolio/Penguin, 2014.

Senge, Peter. *The Fifth Discipline: The Art & Practice of the Learning Organization*. New York: Currency/Doubleday, 1990.

Suzuki, Shunryu. *Zen Mind, Beginner's Mind: Informal Talks on Zen Meditation and Practice*. Boston: Shambhala, 2006.

Van der Kolk, Bessel. *The Body Keeps the Score: Brain, Mind, and Body in the Healing of Trauma*. New York: Penguin Books, 2015.

Wright, Robert. *Why Buddhism Is True: The Science and Philosophy of Meditation and Enlightenment*. New York: Simon & Schuster, 2017.

INDEX

ABOUT THE AUTHOR

Marc Lesser is CEO of ZBA Associates, a company providing mindfulness-based leadership trainings, executive coaching, and keynote talks. He has led trainings at many of the world's leading businesses and organizations, including Google, SAP, Genentech, and Kaiser. He is the cofounder and former CEO of the Search Inside Yourself Leadership Institute, based on a program he helped develop within Google.

Marc was a resident of the San Francisco Zen Center for ten years and former director of Tassajara Zen Mountain Center, and he currently leads Mill Valley Zen, a weekly meditation group. Marc has an MBA degree from New York University and is the author of *Z.B.A. — Zen of Business Administration*, *Less*, and *Know Yourself, Forget Yourself.*

NEW WORLD LIBRARY is dedicated to publishing books and other media that inspire and challenge us to improve the quality of our lives and the world.

We are a socially and environmentally aware company. We recognize that we have an ethical responsibility to our readers, our authors, our staff members, and our planet.

We serve our readers by creating the finest publications possible on personal growth, creativity, spirituality, wellness, and other areas of emerging importance. We serve our authors by working with them to produce and promote quality books that reach a wide audience. We serve New World Library employees with generous benefits, significant profit sharing, and constant encouragement to pursue their most expansive dreams.

Whenever possible, we print our books with soy-based ink on 100 percent postconsumer-waste recycled paper. We power our offices with solar energy and contribute to nonprofit organizations working to make the world a better place for us all.

Our products are available wherever books are sold. Visit our website to download our catalog, subscribe to our e-newsletter, read our blog, and link to authors' websites, videos, and podcasts.

customerservice@newworldlibrary.com
Phone: 415-884-2100 or 800-972-6657
Orders: Ext. 10 • Catalog requests: Ext. 10
Fax: 415-884-2199

www.newworldlibrary.com